Intimate Partner Violence

Effective Procedure, Response and Policy

Intimate Partner Violence

Effective Procedure, Response and Policy

Elicka Peterson Sparks
Appalachian State University
Boone, North Carolina, USA

Kit Gruelle
Utah Domestic Violence Coalition
Salt Lake City, Utah, USA

CRC Press
Taylor & Francis Group
Boca Raton London New York

CRC Press is an imprint of the
Taylor & Francis Group, an **informa** business

CRC Press
Taylor & Francis Group
6000 Broken Sound Parkway NW, Suite 300
Boca Raton, FL 33487-2742

Printed on acid-free paper
Version Date: 20160406

International Standard Book Number-13: 978-1-4987-7359-1 (Paperback)

Library of Congress Cataloging-in-Publication Data

Names: Peterson-Sparks, Elicka, 1967- author. | Gruelle, Kit, author.
Title: Intimate partner violence : effective procedure, response and policy / Elicka Peterson Sparks and Kit Gruelle.
Description: Boca Raton : Taylor & Francis, 2016. | Includes bibliographical references and index.
Identifiers: LCCN 2016009799 | ISBN 9781498773591 (alk. paper)
Subjects: LCSH: Marital violence. | Dating violence. | Family violence. | Family violence--Prevention. | Family violence--Law and legislation.
Classification: LCC HV6626 .P467 2016 | DDC 362.82/92--dc23
LC record available at https://lccn.loc.gov/2016009799

Visit the Taylor & Francis Web site at
http://www.taylorandfrancis.com

and the CRC Press Web site at
http://www.crcpress.com

For Gloria Steinem, all the survivors of
intimate partner violence and the tireless people who
do the hard, necessary work to help them

Contents

Acknowledgments

Elicka—Many people helped, supported and encouraged me in the completion of the research for this book, and I would especially like to thank Maggie, Jessica and Megan Sparks, my parents, Cathy Marcum, Jennifer Kopolow, all the people who do such amazing work in this area, Luna, Spice, Sugar and my colleagues in the Department of Government and Justice Studies at Appalachian State University. I have the best friends and colleagues in the world. Thank you all so much. Finally, thanks to Gloria Steinem for introducing me to Kit. You were right—we definitely needed to know one another. I owe you one.

Kit—I would like to thank all the survivors of domestic and sexual violence I have had the privilege to work with and learn from for the last 30years. Your wisdom, strength and determination never cease to inspire and humble me. I would also like to thank those who have dedicated their lives to doing what they can to address and end this still-misunderstood epidemic. Specifically, I want to thank Jo Sanders, Jane Allen Wilson, Jean Kilpatrick, Glen Hackney and Andrea Batshe, who are so loving to women and children. Janice Reinerth, Amy Page, Beth Davison, Ed Rosenberg and Joyce Powers helped get this old undergraduate through school. And I would also like to thank the late Ellen Pence, our stand-up comedienne and Yoda, all rolled into one, for her immeasurable brilliance. And of course, many thanks to Gloria Steinem for everything, including introducing me to Elicka. We hope that this book helps to illuminate some of the issues that victims and survivors of intimate partner violence are still forced to navigate every day. I would like to dedicate my part of this book to my three kids, Matt, Jason and Noelle. I am so proud to be your mom! I love the three of you so much!

Authors

Elicka Peterson Sparks, PhD, is an associate professor of criminal justice and criminology in the Department of Government and Justice Studies at Appalachian State University in Boone, North Carolina. Dr. Peterson Sparks' research focuses on victimology, the criminogenic impact of religion, domestic violence and homicide. She has published scholarly articles on homicide, domestic violence, sex offending, jury decision making, juvenile justice, actuarial justice, mentoring, police response to intimate partner violence and criminological theory, and her research has appeared in criminological journals such as *Theoretical Criminology, Homicide Studies, Punishment & Society, The Criminal Justice Law Review* and *The Journal of Criminal Justice Education*. Dr. Peterson Sparks is the author of the book, *The Devil You Know: The Surprising Link between Conservative Christianity and Crime*. She has also consulted for numerous media outlets, and on several documentaries, including PBS's *Blind Spot: Murder by Women* and HBO's *Private Violence*.

Kit Gruelle is a survivor of domestic violence and has worked as an advocate for battered women and their children for nearly 30 years. She started her work as a crisis-line volunteer in Durham, North Carolina in the mid-1980s at the Orange–Durham Coalition for Battered Women. In 1995, she created and coordinated the Bridges Program, a coordinated community response (CCR) program, at the Family Violence and Rape Crisis Services in Chatham County, North Carolina. She has also been a subject matter expert (SME) and an instructor for California Peace Officer Standards and Training (POST) since 1997. In 2012, she completed her sociology degree (with a concentration in violence against women) at Appalachian State University. In 2001, she created the documentary film project Private Violence: The Movement against Battering in America. The feature-length, Emmy-nominated film, *Private Violence,* directed by Cynthia Hill, premiered in January 2014 at the Sundance Film Festival and on HBO on October 20, 2014. Kit's article, "Healing From Within: Physicians Responding to Battered Women" is the foreword to *The Physicians Guide to Intimate Partner Abuse* by Drs. Ellen Talliferro and Patricia Salber, and parts of her story were recently included in Marlo Thomas' book *It Ain't Over.*

Introduction

We set out to write a book that is both useful and thought-provoking, and hopefully we've succeeded, because the topic demands it. For too long, the term domestic violence has been used in a manner in which the word "domestic" serves to mitigate the word "violence," making it somehow a lesser form of violence in the minds of many people. Hopefully, after reading this book you will realize that, in reality, nothing could be further from the truth. The consequences of domestic violence are pernicious, complex and far-reaching. Victims and bystanders are killed and seriously injured every day, but beyond that, intimate partner violence also contributes to violence in more nuanced ways, through the children who live it and come to see it as normal, and through other crimes and social issues that have their roots in exposure to violence in the home (teenage pregnancy, runaways, high school dropouts, gang-related activity, juvenile crime, substance abuse, etc.).

In the United States, three victims of domestic violence are murdered every day. Let that sink in for a minute, because it is difficult to grasp. While most people think of homicide as something that is perpetrated by strangers, the risk is far greater that the offender will be known to the victim—often intimately. We do not tend to see that risk as personal, because the vast majority of us believe that the people around us would never hurt us. Domestic violence victims and survivors felt the same way you do in that respect; abusers are skilled at giving the initial impression that they are loving, attentive and even protective rather than dangerous. But while we may know this intellectually, it is tougher to get our heads around the fact that this is something that really could happen to us. Many people who think that domestic violence does not happen to people like them or their family, friends and associates end up victims. Because domestic violence victims feel so stigmatized, many women, even domestic violence victims themselves, work to create space between themselves and the reality of their victimization.*

Why does society reflexively blame victims? If we can find something about a particular kind of victimization that we believe we would never do—from drinking to excess in the case of sexual assault, to becoming involved with an abusive partner in the case of domestic violence—it insulates us from the fear that we might be victimized in that manner ourselves. But the truth is that we're all at risk, no matter what we tell ourselves about how we are somehow immune.

Victim-blaming is extremely prevalent and problematic in the case of domestic violence, as seems to be the case in all crimes perpetrated primarily against female victims. We do not respond to domestic violence in an effective manner, which would mean dealing directly with the source: the abuser and an indifferent society. In this book, your conceptions about the causes and seriousness of domestic violence will be challenged, and you will be given practical advice with respect to helping victims at individual, social and policy levels. We will focus on the source of the abuse and violence: the offenders, and—sad to say in this day and age—a criminal justice system that still has little real regard for the seriousness of intimate terrorism. Far too often, the very system that women turn to for help, in effect, drives the getaway car for the abuser.

In Chapter 1 of this book, the perception that domestic violence is a minor criminal offense relative to other crimes is addressed. Statistics will be presented to support the case that intimate partner violence is both serious and far too common an occurrence, and the information will be augmented by case narratives to provide context and interest. Moreover, the statistics will be presented in a comparative fashion

---

* Leslie Morgan Steiner, *Crazy Love* (New York: St. Martin's Griffin, 2010).

that tends to be more memorable and striking, such as comparing the number of domestic violence-related deaths in a given period to the death toll in the Iraq and Afghanistan wars for that same period. Domestic violence is the root cause for roughly 70%–80% of all hostage-taking and barricade incidents, and a significant portion of public and mass shootings. Few people connect these dots, and it is extremely important for criminal justice professionals and the general public to do so in order for intimate partner violence to garner the concern—and response—it warrants.

In Chapter 2, the concept of coercive control and its central role in domestic violence is presented. The often subtle forms of control abusers use to first gain and then maintain control over their victims are addressed and illustrated using narratives from domestic violence cases. These less-obvious types of control are often more indicative of the risk for serious violence and homicide than many other factors, and are often overlooked by friends, family and criminal justice professionals. Physical violence (including homicide) is the punctuation mark; it is used when other tactics have failed, and is actually a last ditch device that is part of a continuum of tactics used to isolate the victim and maintain the control and position of superiority to which the abuser feels entitled. As such, the fact that victims must be beaten severely to be taken seriously by the criminal justice system has profoundly negative consequences for the victim while giving the abuser the sense that his abuse and violence will be given a pass by the criminal justice system, right up until there is a dead body.

In Chapter 3, the complicated process of leaving violent intimate relationships is explored. The increased risk of homicide when women leave, the complicated nature of love and violence, financial, familial and child-related issues in leaving and how to best help women with respect to getting out are addressed in this section. We will also upend and reframe the age-old, victim-blaming question "Why doesn't she just leave?" and pose a new, more relevant question: "Why does he feel entitled to control, coerce, intimidate and abuse her, and why does society allow him to do it?" When criminal justice professionals truly understand the danger and nuance inherent in the decision to leave, responses to domestic violence will improve dramatically, at the level of the individual professional, the community and at the policy level. The danger is inherent not only for the victim, but also for her family, bystanders, the larger community and law enforcement. Leaving is a process—not an event—and patience with this process is easier when you realize that the woman is in the best position to judge the danger with respect to the timing of her escape.

In Chapter 4, demographic factors in victimization risk for intimate violence are explored, and many of the prevailing notions about where such abuse occurs in society are debunked. Factors such as socioeconomic status, drug and alcohol use, gun ownership and race are addressed. In this discussion, we address reporting issues that have a significant impact on domestic violence statistics.

In Chapter 4, we attempt to cut through some of the myths and misperceptions regarding male victims of intimate partner violence. While men are certainly victims of domestic violence—and any violence is problematic and should be addressed—the seriousness of the harm is far from commensurate with the same violence perpetrated against women. The truth is that it is rare that such violence causes harm anywhere close to that of the violence routinely perpetrated against women, though this low-level violence does take place often enough to warrant discussion. Finally, mandatory arrest policies are discussed in this context with respect to arrests of women for low-level and defensive violence.

Chapter 5 presents a discussion and evaluation of a variety of programs and policies that respond to domestic violence, from shelters, mandatory arrest and restraining orders, to an innovative residential program for domestic violence offenders in Tel Aviv, Israel, called Beit Noam. This also includes a discussion of alternative means to deter chronic and serial batterers who are undeterred by current criminal justice practices, and threat assessment, among other important topics.

In Chapter 6, the underlying social factors impacting societal and criminal justice responses to domestic violence victimization are addressed, and effective means to respond to and counteract misogynistic influences are discussed. Domestic violence must be taken more seriously by both the public and the criminal justice system, and practical steps toward realizing this goal are presented. The United States has a particularly high homicide rate, and domestic violence contributes to this rate significantly. It's a serious problem that receives far too little attention.

After reading this book, you should be well prepared to respond to domestic violence as a law enforcement officer, court official, advocate, shelter, emergency room, protective services worker or educator. You should have a firm grasp on the seriousness of this insidious crime, along with knowledge about how to help victims become survivors. Finally, you should have a strong sense about how to support and create effective policies and programs to both respond to and prevent intimate partner violence.

Many people helped and supported us in writing this book beyond our families and friends, and we are extremely grateful to them. We can never thank you enough for all your love and support. While any errors or omissions are ours alone, many provided excellent theories, information and experience that greatly enhanced the work, not the least of whom are the domestic violence victims and survivors whose stories and pictures ground this book in reality. Without them, this book would be a pale version of itself, and we are enormously grateful for their courage.

Evan Stark's book, *Coercive Control*, is, in our opinion, a must-read for anyone seeking to better understand the dynamics of domestic violence, and we are indebted to him for his important work. If you are looking to dig deeper to gain an even greater understanding of the problem, we strongly recommend you check it out. Lundy Bancroft's book, *Why Does He Do That? Inside the Minds of Angry and Controlling Men*, is also a must-read on the subject. Gloria Steinem provided support and encouragement, as well as feedback that was invaluable to the work. Her example and work in paving the way for such conversations are difficult to overestimate.

This book provides a listing by state of domestic violence resources that can be downloaded from the CRC website (http://www.crcpress.com/product/isbn/9781498773591).

1

Domestic Violence

Far More Serious Than You Think

There are many reasons why domestic violence doesn't strike the chord that it should as a serious form of violent crime. It is difficult to ignore the fact that most victims are women—and children, by extension—in pondering this question, and misogyny and patriarchy play a central role in the dismissive attitude that pervades the issue. The fact that many people see domestic violence as an extension of "fighting" between intimate partners that perhaps got out of hand no doubt adds to the attitudinal malaise. Moreover, the familiar "this-is-none-of-my-business" or "she must have done something to make him angry" belief system isolates her and allows the violence to go undetected in many cases, which lends itself to statistical underreporting as well as the public simply not seeing intimate violence when it might be happening right before them.[1] Reporting is further hampered by legitimate fear on the part of the victims, who may view police involvement as too risky. Despite problems with reporting, domestic violence calls are still the largest category of calls made to the police.[2] Also, for many women, leaving her abuser is the most dangerous thing she can do, so her choice is to stay and live with the violence and abuse or leave and run a much greater risk of being killed by her abuser.[3]

Whatever the reasons, a very serious form of violence is often diminished and viewed as something less serious, and this contributes to perpetuating the problem through a tepid response from the criminal justice system. Victim-blaming is a part of the problem, too, as you will see in Chapters 2 and 3, though that judgment mostly expresses a lack of understanding about the nature of intimate violence. In this chapter, we hope to drive home the fact that domestic violence is extraordinarily serious, and that we cannot afford to minimize the truth about its impact on society.

For the purposes of this book, we will use the National Coalition Against Domestic Violence's (NCADV) definition of domestic violence:

> Domestic violence is the willful intimidation, physical assault, battery, sexual assault, and/or other abusive behavior as part of a systematic pattern of power and control perpetrated by one intimate partner against another. It includes physical violence, sexual violence, threats, and emotional abuse. The frequency and severity of domestic violence can vary dramatically.[4]

Intimate partner violence constitutes 14% of all violent crime in the United States, and it is important to remember that this number is likely far higher due to a number of issues that will be addressed later in this chapter, such as patterned underreporting.[5]

In a national survey, one-fifth of participants disclosed that they were victims of domestic violence, and of those victims, roughly 40% were injured, with 30% of those injuries requiring medical attention.[6] On average, roughly 20 people are victims of physical violence at the hands of an intimate partner in the United States per *minute*.[7] More than three women per *day* are killed by their intimate partners in the United States.[8] One-in-five women experience severe physical violence at the hands of an intimate partner in their lifetime.[9] Make no mistake: Despite the lack of an outcry over this serious social problem, it is a quiet epidemic that results in physical injury, death and severe psychological trauma every minute of every day. The cost of intimate partner violence in dollars has been estimated to exceed $8.3 billion/year.[10]

Domestic violence does not always stay in the home, either. A study of workplace violence occurring between 2003 and 2008 found that 22% of female victims of homicide in the workplace were killed by their intimate or ex-intimate partners.[11] In many cases, colleagues and other bystanders are injured and killed in these homicides, as well.[12] The majority of mass shootings in the United States—homicides in which four or more people are killed in the same incident—are acts of intimate partner or family violence.[13] Often, the fact that these homicides are perpetrated by an estranged husband or boyfriend receives little to no attention in media reports, in part because a workplace shooting is considered more exotic and newsworthy than a domestic homicide, even where bystanders too are murdered.[14] When it comes to murder-suicides, 72% involve an intimate partner and 94% of the homicide victims are women.[15]

The October 2011 mass shooting in Seal Beach, California is a good example of intimate partner violence going public and resulting in the death of eight people (with one other victim shot, but surviving), including the perpetrator's estranged wife, Michelle Fournier. The assailant, Scott Dekraai, was wearing a bullet-proof vest when he walked into the upscale salon where Fournier worked and systematically executed her, three of her colleagues, five clients and a customer of a nearby restaurant in the parking lot.[16] Upon entering the salon, he first shot his ex-wife multiple times, and then turned his weapons on others present in a 2-minute multiple shooting in which he reloaded one of his weapons. According to Dekraai, he had argued with his wife over custody arrangements that morning, leading him to want to kill her. In 2007, a restraining order barring him from possessing handguns had been issued, but had expired by the time of the mass shooting.

In another shooting at a salon, this time in suburban Milwaukee, Radcliffe Haughton, a former Marine, opened fire, killing his estranged wife and two other women, and wounding four others. Just 3 days before the mass murder-suicide, his wife, Zina Haughton, pleaded with the court for protection in a restraining order hearing, saying that her husband would surely kill her, had threatened to throw acid on her face, accused her of cheating on him, and that his jealousy "terrorized her every waking moment."[17] Though the judge issued the order, forbidding Haughton from contact with this wife for the next 4 years and from possessing a handgun, he purchased a .40 caliber gun from a private seller the day before the shooting. Wisconsin law only requires that only dealers must perform background checks on gun buyers. At the hearing, Zina Haughton detailed 20 years of physical violence, and told the judge, "I don't want to die."[18]

The infamous D.C. Sniper case that left 10 people dead in October of 2002 is a chilling example of a spree shooting where domestic violence was an underlying issue—and where the mainstream media never really reported that involvement. Most people have a vague sense that the murders committed by John Allen Muhammad and Lee Boyd Malvo were motivated by racial hatred directed against white people, or simply a murderous rampage, and the media failed to connect the case back to the control and emotional abuse levelled at Mildred Muhammad, John Allen Muhammad's estranged wife, despite the fact that the first victim was mistakenly believed to be Isa Farrington Nichols—a woman who had provided shelter for Mildred Muhammad and her children while the marriage was still intact. John Allen Muhammad had become so verbally and emotionally abusive and controlling that Mildred had left him and filed for divorce. As is so often the case, that was when the real terrorism started. An educated woman and businessperson, Mildred could hardly feed herself and her children, found herself in a shelter, had her children taken away by her husband for 18 months, and feared for her life as the threats from John Allen Muhammad escalated.[19] "It began as a domestic dispute between a man and his wife," according to Nichols, who was spared because she was not at home when Malvo came knocking on her door. Sadly, her 21-year-old niece was at the home, and was killed instead.[20]

On Black Friday of 2014, Marcus Dee shot his ex-girlfriend, Nadia Ezaldein, in a crowded Nordstrom's Department Store in Chicago, then turned the gun on himself in an attempted murder-suicide. He was declared dead at the scene, but the victim, who was a student and seasonal employee of the store, was transported to the hospital in critical condition before dying. The police called the incident "domestic-related."[21] Subsequent coverage revealed she was killed on her 22nd birthday, and had left Dee after he put a gun in her mouth in a violent incident that took place in December of 2013, and which resulted in her hospitalization. Her family reported that the incident had taken place after months of "psychological torment" and physical abuse. Nadia and her siblings had received threatening phone calls, forcing her to change her number three times, her sister was beaten up by Dee and left with a fractured jaw, and Dee had been stalking her.[22] Her sister tried to obtain an Order of Protection for her prior to the murder, but the judge refused because Nadia was not present at the hearing, though her sister explained that she was too afraid to show up.[23] Her family had flown in to Chicago to throw a surprise birthday party for her the day she was murdered. Sadly, such examples are extremely easy to come by.

To put all of this in greater perspective, between August 10, 2001 and June 6, 2012, the number of American soldiers who were killed in Iraq and Afghanistan was 6838. In the United States, the number of women killed by their intimate or ex-intimate partners during that same period was 11,766.[24] Let that sink in a bit: More women were killed by their intimate and ex-intimate partners than soldiers who died in the war. Further, sexual violence is prevalent in cases where there is physical abuse, as well, though studies show that the sexual violence is even less likely to be reported to police.[25] We have a serious problem, and it is a well-kept secret in terms of public awareness. Suffice it to say that it is a gross understatement that far too many people are suffering and dying due to intimate partner violence.

On average, 46 women are shot to death by their current or ex-intimate partner every *month* in the United States.[26] Including all weapons, roughly 1400 women die of intimate partner homicides each year.[27] Women are nine times more likely to be killed by an intimate partner than a stranger.[28] Intimate partner homicides account for 14% of all homicides perpetrated in the United States, and 70% of them feature a female victim.[29] From 1998 to 2002, 25% of all murders were committed by a family member of the victim, and 11% of all crimes—not just homicides—were considered crimes of domestic violence.[30] The most important risk factor for intimate partner violence is prior violence within the relationship: Approximately 67%–75% of all such murders feature a history of abuse against the female partner.[31] We could easily go on, but statistics tend to have a diminishing return with respect to impact.

This is a crime that impacts children at a disproportionately high rate relative to most other violent crimes, as well, which adds significantly to the damage and harm caused by these offenses. Even where children are not victimized directly along with the intimate partner, witnessing such violence has a profound effect on their social, cognitive and physical development.[32] In 2002, it was estimated that 3.2 million children witness domestic violence every year.[33] Children who have witnessed domestic violence are at greater risk for anxiety and depression, as well as negative behaviors such as lying, bullying, cheating and fighting. Moreover, they are more likely to be disobedient, exhibit poor school performance and difficulty in relationships with others.[34]

Children who witness intimate partner violence tend to display inappropriate attitudes about using violence to resolve conflicts, and indicate a greater willingness to engage in violence themselves.[35] There are many negative, age-specific impacts on children, including a higher rate of risk-taking and antisocial behaviors such as truancy, substance abuse, early sexual activity and delinquency for adolescents.[36] The impact is profound and the effects lasting, rippling out as damage to these individuals and society that is a direct result of intimate partner violence. In fact, boys who witness intimate partner violence growing up are twice as likely as boys who do not experience such violence to perpetrate violence against their own intimate partners and children when they reach adulthood.[37] The physical, psychological and developmental effects of domestic violence on children can be severe and long lasting, and children who witness violence between their parents without suffering physical harm themselves suffer effects similar to those experiencing direct physical abuse.[38]

It is often difficult to estimate the impact of witnessing intimate partner violence because there is such considerable overlap between domestic violence and child abuse; estimates hold that between 30% and 60% of intimate partner violence offenders abuse children in the household, as well.[39] As such, it is often challenging to discern the impact from each type of trauma from one another. Mothers who are dealing with intimate partner violence are parenting from an extremely stressful place, which also takes a toll on children, who are stressed by the situation themselves.[40]

The cumulative effects on individuals and society are almost incalculable. The intimate partner homicide rate in the United States is higher than many countries' total homicide rates—and yet we hear very little about domestic violence. We see story after story in which women die at the hands of their intimate and ex-intimate partners without seeming to notice that the common feature in these crimes is domestic violence.[41] While we have started to move past notions that domestic violence is a "mind-your-own-business" proposition, the issue is still not treated as seriously as is warranted, in part due to patriarchy, lingering notions about lover's spats, the idea that such violence is unilateral, religious messages about loving, honoring and obeying a husband, and a host of other influences that relegate intimate partner violence to a largely invisible crisis outside of feminist circles.

There is also a heap of judgment when it comes to domestic violence. People tend to believe the solution is simple: A woman just has to leave her abuser to solve the problem. We firmly believe that we would never let anyone treat us that way, so empathy is slow in coming, or nonexistent. Women are held responsible for addressing the problem—not men, the community, law enforcement, or a culture of male privilege and dominance.[42] Despite the information that domestic violence crosses all socioeconomic lines being widely disseminated, the belief that it is solely a lower class phenomenon persists.[43] Intimate partner violence is not just a personal problem that is specific to a few unfortunate women; it is a serious social problem that persists in part because of public misconceptions.[44]

In Chapter 2, you will learn about the meat and potatoes of intimate partner violence—the aspect of abuse that few outside of domestic violence advocacy circles understand that is an issue central to the problem: Domestic violence is really a form of terrorism, committed in the name of love, family, habit, male entitlement, hierarchy, faith and fear of losing control.

What You Can Do

- Speak out about the problem. It is vitally important that people start to see domestic violence for what it is—an extremely serious violent crime.
- If you see a news story involving domestic violence that seems to minimize the involvement of domestic violence or blames the victim, contact the news provider and issue a complaint.
- Start a petition directed at media outlets demanding more substantial coverage of the issue.
- Know what services your local domestic violence prevention program has to offer. At a minimum, they should offer support groups for women and children, emergency crisis counseling

via a hotline, shelter, court advocacy for civil and criminal court, community education, offender treatment programs (or be able to refer him to a local program) and school-based prevention programs. All services (except for the offender treatment programs) are free or sliding scale. All support services for victim and the children are confidential.

- Write to media outlets and encourage them to take this issue on.
- Write letters to the editor.
- Inform your friends and family about the seriousness of the issue.
- Take to the Internet to get the message out there.
- Contact your legislators about focusing attention on this issue.
- If you hear someone joking about domestic violence, let them know it is not a joking matter, but a crime that touches (at least) one out of every four women in the United States.
- If you see intimate partner violence taking place, don't ignore it. Use the lists provided in this book to respond. Ignoring the problem makes it invisible, empowers the abuser—and makes victims feel invisible, marginalized and more vulnerable. She needs to know that domestic violence is wrong and that it is NOT her fault. She must also know that she has resources and a support system in her community that can help her look critically at what is happening. Once she knows she is not alone, things can begin to change for her and the children, and for him, if he is willing to take responsibility for his choice to be abusive, controlling and violent.

Discussion Ideas

1. Is it possible to change patriarchal conceptions that violence against women in these situations is less serious than violence against men? How might that end be achieved?
2. What needs to happen to make intimate partner more visible?
3. Were you aware that domestic violence results in so many homicides prior to reading this chapter? Why or why not?
4. For one week, have everyone in this group try to track intimate partner violence in the news. Read beyond the headlines, looking for clues such as the word "estranged" or "former" or

"ex" to determine the root of violent events. Discuss what you find. Would you have noticed these events as being related to intimate partner violence prior to doing this assignment? Why or why not? Did this change your perception about the size of this problem?

5. Why do we even put intimate partner homicide in a category that feels different from plain old "homicide"?

References and Notes

1. J. Campbell, S. L. Martin, K. E. Moracco, J. A. Manganello, and R. J. Macy, Survey data sets pertinent to the study of intimate partner violence and health, *Trauma, Violence and Abuse* 7; 2006: 7–18.
2. D. Gamache, J. L. Edleson, and M. D. Schock, Coordinated police, judicial and social services response to woman battering: A multiple-baseline evaluation across three communities, in *Coping with Family Violence: Research and Policy Perspectives*, eds. G. T. Hotaling, D. Finkelhor, J. T. Kirkpatrick, and M. A. Straus (Newbury Park, CA: Sage, 1988), 193–211; J. E. Hendricks and C. S. Hendricks, eds., *Crisis Intervention in Criminal Justice and Social Services*, 5th ed. (Springfield, IL: Charles C. Thomas Publishers, 2014). It should be noted that many domestic violence calls are not for actions that could be charged as crimes.
3. See Chapter 3.
4. The National Coalition Against Domestic Violence is a great resource for reliable information about intimate partner violence. Check them out at http://www.ncadv.org.
5. R. E. Morgan and J. L. Truman, *Nonfatal Domestic Violence, 2003–2012* (Washington, DC: U.S. Department of Justice, 2014), http://www.bjs.gov/index.cfm?ty=pbdetail&iid=4984 (accessed December 6, 2014); S. M. Catalano, *Intimate Partner Violence in the United States* (Washington, DC: U.S. Department of Justice, 2012), http://www.bjs.gov/content/pub/pdf/ipv9310.pdf (accessed February 15, 2015).
6. H. Y. Lee, E. Park, and E. Lightfoot, When does a battered woman seek help from the police? The role of battered women's functionality, *Journal of Family Violence* 25; 2010: 195–204.
7. M. C. Black, K. C. Basile, M. J. Breiding, S. G. Smith, M. L. Walters, M. T. Merrick, J. Chen, and M. R. Stevens, *The National Intimate Partner and Sexual Violence Survey: 2010 Summary Report* (National Center for Injury Prevention and Control. Atlanta, GA: Centers for Disease Control and Prevention, 2011), http://www.cdc.gov/violenceprevention/pdf/nisvs_report2010-a.pdf (accessed February 12, 2015).
8. S. M. Catalano, *Intimate Partner Violence in the United States* (Washington, DC: U.S. Department of Justice, 2012), http://www.bjs.gov/content/pub/pdf/ipv9310.pdf (accessed February 15, 2015).

9. Ibid.
10. E. F. Rothman, J. Hathaway, A. Stidsen, and H. F. de Vries, How employment helps female victims of intimate partner abuse: A qualitative study, *Journal of Occupational Health Psychology* 12; 2007: 136–43.
11. H. M. Tiesman, K. K. Gurka, S. Konda, J. H. Coben, and H. E. Amandus, Workplace homicides among U.S. women: The role of intimate partner violence, *Annals of Epidemiology* 22; 2012: 277–84.
12. Ibid. This is certainly not to imply that other deaths are necessary to take this problem seriously.
13. Y. Crasso, My sister's keeper: Working to reduce domestic violence and gun violence, *Women's Health Activist* 39; 2014: 1–5.
14. S. Alhabib, U. Nur, and R. Jones, Domestic violence against women: Systematic review of prevalence studies, *Journal of Family Violence* 25; 2010: 369–82.
15. Violence Policy Center, *American Roulette: Murder-Suicide in the United States*, 4th ed. (Washington, DC: Violence Policy Center, 2012), http://www.vpc.org/press/1205amroul.htm (accessed May 20, 2015).
16. T. Bloom, Scott Dekraai pleads guilty in seal beach salon mass shooting, *KTLA 5 News*, May 2, 2014, http://ktla.com/2014/05/02/accused-seal-beach-salon-shooter-expected-to-plead-guilty/ (accessed May 20, 2015).
17. L. Mungin, Wisconsin spa shooting: Wife told court 'I Don't Want to Die.' *CNN.com*, October 23, 2012, http://www.cnn.com/2012/10/23/justice/wisconsin-shooting/ (accessed February 5, 2015).
18. Ibid.
19. S. Atkinson, Wife of D.C. Sniper tells the story you never heard: Domestic assault was the root cause of shootings, *MLive—The Flint Journal*, November 15, 2012, http://www.mlive.com/entertainment/flint/index.ssf/2012/11/wife_of_dc_sniper_tells_the_st.html (accessed January 3, 2015).
20. S. Adem, D.C. Sniper's first target says killing spree grew from domestic violence, *Howard University News Service*, November 10, 2009, http://www.hunewsservice.com/news/view.php/54040/DC-Snipers-1st-Target-Says-Killing-Spree (accessed December 22, 2014).
21. W. Robinson, Man shoots ex-girlfriend at Nordstrom cosmetics counter before killing himself on Black Friday, *Mail Online News*, November 29, 2014, http://www.dailymail.co.uk/news/article-2853803/Man-shoots-ex-girlfriend-counter-cosmetics-department-busy-Nordstrom-store-killing-himself.html (accessed December 4, 2015).
22. W. Robinson, Student, 22, who was shot dead by Stalker ex-boyfriend in Nordstrom on Black Friday 'Had Split Up with Him after He Hospitalized Her by Putting a Gun in Her Mouth', *Mail Online News*, November 30, 2014, http://www.dailymail.co.uk/news/article-2854592/Woman-shot-ex-boyfriend-counter-Nordstrom-Black-Friday-dies-family-reveal-victim-went-months-psychological-torment-hands-suspect.html (accessed December 4, 2015).

23. J. Gorner, Nordstrom slaying victim too 'scared' to file for Order of Protection, *Chicago Tribune*, December 2, 2014, http://www.chicagotribune.com/news/ct-nordstrom-shooting-met-1202–20141201-story.html (accessed December 4, 2015).
24. Figures from the U.S. Bureau of Justice Statistics and U.S. Department of Defense. This total includes the American death count for Operation Iraqi Freedom (later called Operation New Dawn)—4491 deaths, and Operation Enduring Freedom—2347 (which includes civilian Defense Department employees and another 134 Americans who died outside Afghanistan in war-related incidences).
25. J. McFarlane and A. Malecha, *Sexual Assault among Intimates: Frequency, Consequences and Treatments, Final Report* (Washington, DC: U.S. Department of Justice, 2005).
26. Y. Crasso, My sister's keeper: Working to reduce domestic violence and gun violence, *Women's Health Activist* 39; 2014: 1–5.
27. J. S. Wilson, and N. Websdale, Domestic violence fatality review teams: An interprofessional model to reduce deaths, *Journal of Interprofessional Care* 20; 2006: 535–44.
28. J. C. Campbell, N. Glass, P. W. Sharps, K. Laughon, and T. Bloom, Intimate partner homicide, *Trauma, Violence and Abuse* 8; 2007: 246–69.
29. S. G. Smith, K. A. Fowler, and P. H. Niolon, Intimate partner homicide and corollary victims in 16 states: National violent death reporting system, *American Journal of Public Health* 104; 2014: 461–8, http://www.researchgate.net/profile/Sharon_Smith19/publication/259768650_Intimate_Partner_Homicide_and_Corollary_Victims_in_16_States_National_Violent_Death_Reporting_System_2003-2009/links/5422b3540cf238c6ea6ae188.pdf (accessed November 6, 2014).
30. T. N. Sulak, T. F. Saxon, and D. Fearon, Applying the theory of reasoned action to domestic violence reporting behavior, *Journal of Women's Health* 20; 2014: 1743–9.
31. J. C. Campbell, N. Glass, P. W. Sharps, K. Laughon, and T. Bloom, Intimate partner homicide, *Trauma, Violence & Abuse* 8; 2007: 246–69; C. Diem and J. M. Pizarro, Social structure and family homicides, *Journal of Family Violence* 25; 2010: 521–32.
32. J. M. Attala, K. Bauza, H. Pratt, and D. Viera, Integrative review of effects on children of witnessing domestic violence, *Issues in Comprehensive Pediatric Nursing* 18; 1995: 163–72; J. R. Kolbo, E. H. Blakely, and D. Engleman, Children who witness domestic violence: A review of empirical literature, *Interpersonal Violence* 11; 1996: 281–93.
33. M. M. Stiles, Witnessing domestic violence: The effect on children, *American Family Physician* 66; 2002: 2052–67.
34. Ibid.
35. P. G. Jaffe, D. J. Hurley, and D. Wolfe, Children's observations of violence: I. Critical issues in child development and intervention planning, *Canadian Journal of Psychiatry* 35; 1990: 466–70; P. G. Jaffe, D. Wolfe, S. Wilson, and L. Zak, Similarities in behavioral and social maladjustment among child victims and witnesses to family violence,

American Journal of Orthopsychiatry 56; 1996: 142–45; S. Spaccarelli, J. D. Coatsworth, and B. S. Bowden, Exposure to serious family violence among incarcerated boys: Its association with violent offending and potential mediating variables, *Violence and Victims* 10; 1995: 163–82.

36. M. H. Rhea, K. H. Chafey, V. A. Dohner, and R. Terragno, The silent victims of domestic violence—Who will speak? *Journal of Adolescent Psychiatric Nursing* 9; 1996: 7–15; A. H. Maker, M. Kemmelmeier, and C. Peterson, Long-term psychological consequences in women of witnessing parental physical conflict and experiencing abuse in childhood, *Journal of Interpersonal Violence* 13; 1998: 574–89.
37. M. A. Straus and R. J. Gelles, *Physical Violence in American Families: Risk Factors and Adaptations to Violence in 8,145 Families* (New York: Transaction Publishers, 1989).
38. S. Horley, Addressing domestic violence through support and prevention, *British Journal of School Nursing* 9; 2014: 35–7.
39. J. L. Edelson, The overlap between child maltreatment and woman battering, *Violence Against Women* 5; 1999: 134–54, http://hbftpartnership.com/documents/uploadResources/ChildMLRX-Edleson1999.pdf (accessed September 26, 2014).
40. Ibid.
41. K. Buckler and L. Travis, Assessing the newsworthiness of homicide events, *Journal of Criminal Justice and Popular Culture* 12; 2005: 1–25, http://www.albany.edu/scj/jcjpc/vol12is1/buckler.pdf (accessed April 18, 2015). We will address women as perpetrators of domestic violence in Chapter 4, but as better than 85% of victims are women, we will address this as a women's issue in the rest of the book.
42. T. B. Bent-Goodley, Culture and domestic violence, *Journal of Interpersonal Violence* 20; 2005: 195–203.
43. Socioeconomic status will be discussed in greater depth in Chapter 4. A. L. Horton, M. M. Wilkins, and W. Wright, Women who ended abuse: What religious leaders and religion did for these victims, in *Abuse and Religion: When Praying Isn't Enough*, eds. A. L. Horton and J. A. Williamson (Lexington, MA: Lexington Books, 1988), 235–46.
44. J. M. Cohen, Private violence and public obligation: The fulcrum of reason, in *The Public Nature of Private Violence: The Discovery of Domestic Abuse*, eds. M. Fineman and R. Mykitiuk (New York: Routledge, 1994), 349–82.

2
The Invisible Tactics of Control

The police respond to an intimate partner violence call and find a victim who has obviously been beaten, and is badly shaken. The officers separate the offender and victim to talk with them, and the officer talking with the victim feels he's making some headway in getting the victim to open up. In the course of this exchange, the offender tells the other officer that he needs to go to the bathroom. When he comes out of the bathroom, he walks through the living room carrying a hand towel in view of the other officer and victim. The victim sees him, suddenly becomes less cooperative with the officer, and is visibly afraid. The officer, who has received special training in handling domestic violence incidents and is very intuitive, quietly asks the victim what just happened. The victim shares that the offender puts a towel over her face and then hits her through the towel. If not for a perceptive police officer, this exchange would have gone completely unnoticed, and the victim's sudden reluctance to talk would not have been viewed for what it was—a completely rational and understandable response to a coded but clear threat.

One of the hardest things for people to understand about intimate partner violence is the aspect of control and coercion on the part of abusers. In part, this is because such control is hidden, and much of it consists of signals abusers send to their victims that are extremely effective in keeping her in line, but too subtle for outsiders to notice unless they are trained to look for them. Perpetrators control minute details in the lives of victims, reinforcing superior and subordinate positions in the relationship. This deepens the fear of resisting or attempting to escape, and leaves victims trapped in a situation that amounts to an intimate form of terrorism.[1]

The forms of coercion and control employed are as varied as the individuals themselves. One perpetrator insisted that his victim use her phone to take a picture of each aisle and text it to him as she shopped for groceries with the threat of physical violence when she got home if she "failed" to comply with his demands, ensuring total control over her even in his absence. Another perpetrator, who happened to be in law enforcement himself, insisted that his wife get on the scale each day, and weigh exactly the same each morning. Another offender required his victim to buy salted peanuts and wash the salt off the peanuts to put on his ice cream each night. If he found residual salt on the peanuts, he beat her as punishment for her failure. Again, the variations are endless, but the goal is the same: to exert and maintain total control over the victim.[2]

Types of Intimate Control

Abusive relationships rarely if ever start out that way.[3] Women consistently characterize eventual abusers as being the nicest guy they'd ever met at the beginning of the courtship. This is an integral part of the issue that develops: If she sees him as such a nice guy, and if others do as well, when the abusive and controlling behavior begins, she tends to look inward for cues and clues to reconcile the new reality of the relationship with the old. This is the beginning of a confusing, downward spiral for the victim as she seeks to understand the new reality of the relationship. Often, she is trying to make sense of what is happening behind the scenes while friends and family only see the initial behavior of the perpetrator—the proverbial nicest guy you'd ever want to meet.

As the relationship progresses, there are some common types of intimate control that come into play. A prime example is the look. The look is a method of control in which the offender stares the victim down in a manner that promises violence if his will is not carried out. It is particularly effective in silencing victims in the presence of potential interlopers, such as police. A meaningful stare—the meaning most often some variation of "I will hurt/kill you if you tell on me"—is enough to keep victims silent, even once separated from the offender. The look has the benefit of going unnoticed by bystanders, who frequently have no idea that a threatening communication has even transpired between the offender and victim. It is all the more effective for its stealth, which reinforces the victim's feeling that nobody understands or will be able to help them. Parents use the look to great effect in correcting children because it works: Imagine if that look included the threat of violence rather than the threat of a reasonable punishment for misbehavior.

Coded gestures are another common means of exerting nonviolent control over a victim. Sometimes the gestures are not subtle, as in the case of an offender making a covert fist to threaten a victim, but often they represent a specific instance of prior abuse to the victim, as in the real example with the hand towel at the beginning of the chapter. Because outsiders cannot possibly know the history behind many of these gestures, the best course of action is to watch offenders closely for any gestures that seem unusual, and then check in with the victim about anything fitting that description. If you are aware that offenders are likely trying to communicate a threat, it is far easier to detect it, even where the exact nature of the threat is not clear to you. Ask the victim to explain what is transpiring and what it means between her and the perpetrator. The victim is the *expert* in what is occurring—encourage her to talk, remind her that you appreciate that such violence and control can be hard to talk about, and then *listen to her.*

Nonviolent coercion also includes annihilating the victim's sense of self and self-esteem. The goal is to make the victim feel lucky to even have the offender in an intimate partnership, and to reinforce the idea that she deserves the treatment she receives from him.[4] This type of control has the added benefit of making the victim believe that nobody will be interested in helping her. The perpetrator berating a victim as stupid, unattractive and the like all add to a sense of isolation and dependence. Remember, these messages are coming from someone with whom she has had a very loving relationship at some point, so this is part of why it is all so confusing to her. In helping victims of intimate violence, countering these negative messages is important.[5] After the victim's self-esteem has been minimized, it is not uncommon for the perpetrator to further control her through the threat of leaving.[6,7]

Perhaps the most widely known means of control is isolation from family, friends and other potential avenues for support. Restricting a victim's autonomy to engage in relationships where others might have influence is a powerful way to control a person, as it eliminates alternate, positive messages and potential help in one stroke.[8] Perpetrators are able to do this fairly easily at the beginning of a relationship, as spending a lot of time with one another is pretty normal when a relationship is new, and calls to exclude others are easy to mask as a flattering desire to be alone with the other person. The difference is that the normal process of socializing with others does not resume after the courtship/grooming phase of the relationship is over. It is also a way for him to test her, to understand whom she maintains close relationships with so that he can start to do what he feels is necessary to compromise those relationships. Isolation is one of the key goals.

Charm is another weapon in the arsenal of control tactics used by perpetrators, and it receives little attention relative to the frequency of its use. Offenders are often skilled at turning on the charm when it is necessary to maintain control over their partner, especially in the earlier stages.[9] If the woman starts to have doubts about the dynamics in the relationship, the perpetrator is able to read that doubt and respond with reassuring words and behaviors that remind her of who he was at the beginning of their relationship and/or make her question her perception of the situation. Offenders use their charisma, charm, wiles and any other tactic that is successful to keep their victim off-balance and, ultimately, stuck in the violent relationship.

Yet another method used to control victims is to control perceptions about the victim. Portraying the victim as hysterical, unstable, a liar, abusive, dramatic, unfaithful, "on the rag," a drunk or drug addict and the like to others makes it more difficult for victims to get the help they need from outside of the relationship. It also creates the opportunity for him to connect and bond with law enforcement, undermining her ability to be heard and respected by them and others in the criminal justice system. This may be the one and only chance she will have to reach out for help, so if she believes that law enforcement officers are viewing her negatively, she may never call for help again. Her credibility is compromised before she even seeks help, and she is likely aware of that. When outsiders are unsure who is telling the truth, it makes it easy to stand by instead of getting involved, feeling they have a "he said/she said" situation on their hands that might be unilateral. Perpetrators may also use their status in the community to remind the victim that "no one will ever believe you." Casting doubt on the victim is thus an effective method to keep potential intervention at bay.

Financial control is another mechanism employed by perpetrators. Getting their partners to quit their jobs, or simply keeping tight control over the family budget to the extent that women have no access to financial resources is an effective way to block the exit of a partner, particularly where children are involved. Offenders often dole out money for purchases such as groceries, and keep careful track of victims' spending. It is extremely difficult to contemplate leaving if one is unable to afford basic necessities.

Perpetrators also use a host of excuses to control their victims. They implant ideas that encourage women to hang on in the relationship out of pity or hope when fear alone fails to do the trick. Offenders use a variety of these justifications and rationalizations to excuse their abusive behavior, but a couple are extremely common. Playing on the sympathy of the victim, perpetrators often point to their own abusive or dysfunctional upbringing as the reason they abuse. While there is a strong correlation between witnessing early abuse and later perpetration of violence in the family, it is not a causative relationship; the perpetrator is still choosing to offend against the victim.[10] Another common ploy is to portray the abusive behavior as the occasional loss of control by an otherwise good man. Women naturally seek to find excuses too; they don't want to believe the "wonderful man" they fell in love with is capable of this abusive and controlling behavior.

This ploy also serves to place the responsibility for the violence on the victim through the suggestion that her actions spurred the loss of control. Intimate partner violence perpetrators choose to ramp up the abusive tactics when their nonviolent forms of control and coercion have failed—physical abuse is often their last-ditch effort to bring the victim to heel. But physical violence is a tactic to renew their hold over a victim rather than a true loss of control in most cases, and in no case is it the action of a good man.

Victims are often overwhelmed by the barrage of strategies employed by perpetrators to keep them in the relationship and under the full control of the offender. Adding to this untenable situation is the fact that these relationships are complicated. It would be far easier for women to leave if offenders were always abusive, but that is rarely the case. Sometimes abusers are thoughtful and loving. Sometimes abusers are good parents to children. Sometimes abusers are good providers (or simply the sole source of support). And perhaps most importantly, victims fell in love with the abuser, which is both confusing and frightening.

Nobody thinks that they are capable of falling in love with someone who hurts them badly, so searching for alternative explanations is natural. Most battered women say, "I just want the violence to stop, and I want him to go back to being the way he was when we first got together." Rather than questioning him, the victim begins to question herself, her actions and her ability to make sound decisions.

It is so frightening to think yourself incapable of seeing someone for who they really are that you protect yourself from that ideation by making excuses for the offender. Perpetrators are skilled at hiding who they are in the beginning of a new relationship, often seeming for all the world like a fantastic catch. Outsiders often view the offender as a terrific guy, adding to the sense of confusion and doubt on the part of the victim. This brings about an important point to remember: Perpetrators are most often completely capable of controlling themselves in the presence of others. Moreover, if they are able to avoid becoming physically violent outside of the home, they are capable of avoiding it inside the home. They simply choose not to do so.

Perpetrators' Excuses and Justifications for Violence and Control

There are about as many excuses and justifications used to rationalize intimate partner violence and coercion as there are types of control. Most of them are offered up by the offenders themselves, and yet they are accepted as valid and passed along in our culture as though they are the *causes* of this type of violence. One of the best ways to separate causes from excuses is to simply think about whether the supposed cause can take place without intimate partner violence following. Drinking is one such excuse. People drink all the time without committing intimate partner violence, but drinking is often used as an excuse for committing intimate partner violence. Just as people choose whether or not to get behind the wheel after they've had too much to drink, so too do offenders choose whether to perpetrate violence against their partners or ex-partners. When you start assessing so-called reasons for domestic violence through this lens, you quickly see that they are not the cause. Quite simply, the offender, and the way the offender thinks about their intimate partner, is the only condition that needs to exist for violence and control to occur.

It's a Woman's Fault

A common excuse for domestic violence places the blame on the victim, or on another woman in the perpetrator's past. One of the most common versions of this excuse is that a former intimate partner "made him like this" through a variety of misbehavior that now triggers him in his current relationship. The former girlfriend cheated on him, so he cannot help being jealous and possessive. The former wife had him arrested out of vindictiveness, so he goes crazy when the current partner suggests that his behavior is abusive. The ex was controlling, turned the children against him, never letting him know where she was, would not let him have what he wanted, never wanted to have sex, kept close tabs on him, did not keep their home clean, etc.

Whatever the perpetrator says the ex-partner did or did not do is then used as the justification for abuse in the current relationship. Almost without fail, if the characteristic or behavior of an ex is being used as an excuse for bad behavior in the current relationship, the information the offender is sharing about the earlier relationship is a distortion. One good way to get to the bottom of this type of excuse is to track down the former partner and ask for her side of the story. Chances are good that she was abused by the perpetrator, as well. Finally, here is something to think about with respect to this justification: Women are even more likely than men to have abusive relationships in their past, but do not tend to use this as an excuse to justify abusive behavior. As such, if past relationships were really the cause of abuse, women would be far more likely to abuse their partners than men.

The next most likely woman to take the blame for the offender's violence and control is his mother. In this excuse, the perpetrator hates women because his mother did horrible things to him to make him hate women.[11] However, there are a number of problems with this notion of why men are abusive. Most importantly, it cannot account for the fact that intimate perpetrators often have a good number of prosocial relationships with other women in their lives (sisters, colleagues, mothers, and friends). They are able to refrain from violence in those relationships, and the relationships themselves suggest that there is no overreaching hatred of women present.

While male perpetrators may disrespect and devalue women—sometimes covertly—this is more a manifestation of cultural values than past personal experiences.[12] Additionally, it is telling that men with abusive mothers are less likely to become abusers themselves than those with abusive fathers. The cultural transmission of selfishness and ideas about women existing to cater to their needs is far more likely the culprit than an overbearing or abusive mother.

Finally, the victim herself is to blame. He is violent because he feels so strongly about her, and these feelings cause his behavior. Nobody can get under his skin like she does and get him so upset—this is why he only offends against her. This excuse taps into unhealthy societal notions that passion and aggression are somehow interwoven.[13] His great love for her causes him to hurt her. The main problem with this rationalization is that feelings do not directly cause behavior, except in cases of those with severe psychological problems. People react in a variety of ways to feelings; one person might have a glass of wine in response to strong feelings, another might have a good cry, and yet another might choose a trip to the gym to deal with strong emotions. We *choose* how we will behave in response to strong feelings. This is evident in abusive men who use this excuse, yet only seem to act on those feelings in a private setting.

He Was or Is Abused Himself

Another common excuse for victimizing intimate partners is that the perpetrator was abused as a child. For starters, men who perpetrate violence against other *men* are more likely to have been abused than those who perpetrate violence against *women*.[14] The only exception to this is offenders who use extreme violence against their female victims—they are more likely to have been abused.[15] But the history of abuse does not cause the abuse even in those cases (though it can make it worse). This excuse for violence has the added benefit of instilling sympathy in others for his plight, and offenders get a lot of mileage out of sympathy as a mechanism for controlling their partners. Overall, men who experienced or witnessed abuse as children should be more empathetic to victims—not less—and many are more empathetic and would never abuse a woman.

This abuse excuse is sometimes extended to apply to people currently abusing the perpetrator, such as a boss. The idea here is that the poor offender comes home and takes it out on his family because it is the one place where he has power and control. Aside from the fact that many abusers are successful men with good relationships with their bosses—or who are the boss—Lundy Bancroft makes a terrific point in noting that, in 15 years of practice with perpetrators, he has never had an offender who's behavior at home improved in response to an improvement in their job situation.[16]

He Just Needs Help

In this category of excuse, the offender simply needs skills or intervention to address a variety of issues he might have. Most of these issues are pulled straight from the realm of pop psychology, but are widely believed to be causes of domestic violence. The most common of these justifications is that the perpetrator suffers from low self-esteem. He feels bad about himself, and this somehow results in his making others feel worse about themselves, as well. This is another especially convenient excuse for offenders, because it leads to their receiving special treatment from their partners in an attempt to buttress their supposedly flagging sense of self-worth.

This excuse, like all the others, is rubbish. If anything, abusive men tend to have too high an opinion of themselves, and too low an opinion of their victims. When victims and others try to boost his self-esteem, he simply grows to expect more and more deference. There is no satiation point; women are simply raising the bar on themselves to give the offender preferential treatment to assuage their supposed lack of self-worth. The more attention the perpetrator receives, the more he demands. The situation is not sustainable. Luckily, as this is not the reason he is offending, it is not necessary to try to cater to him emotionally in this manner. The offender may occasionally feel bad about himself in light of his abusive behavior, but these moments are the result of his abusive behavior, not the cause of it. Finally, if low self-esteem caused people to be abusive, then victims of domestic violence would have the highest likelihood of abusing their partner.

Poor communication, conflict resolution skills or stress management are also viewed as the culprit by many people, and used as justifications by offenders. These explanations have a lot of intuitive appeal. After all, they are not communicating verbally in an appropriate manner when they scream or use violence, nor does this represent a good means of conflict resolution. Finally, they seem to explode in stress over the slightest provocation, such as their laundry not being folded the way they like it. Again, this is rubbish, and the proof is once again found in the offenders' behavior outside of the home. The vast majority of perpetrators are perfectly capable of communicating, resolving conflicts and managing their stress out in the world; they simply choose not to use those skills with their intimate partner.[17]

Fears of abandonment and intimacy are also trotted out as excuses for intimate partner violence. Once again, the offenders' behavior makes this justification seem plausible at first blush. Perpetrators are almost always jealous and possessive, which seems to give credence to a fear of abandonment underlying the violent behavior. The fear of intimacy argument makes use of stereotypes of men as particularly prone to having a fear of intimacy, and it gains strength through explaining why most perpetrators focus their violent attentions exclusively on their intimate partner.

But once again, the problem with these excuses and supposed causes of intimate partner violence become clear when you take a step back from the violence and control and gain some context and perspective. If fear of intimacy and abandonment cause the violence, why do we not see more women abusing men? If abuse is used to mediate intimacy, why do these offenders so often abuse at times that are not intimate at all. At the end of the day, many men and women fear intimacy and abandonment, but do not commit intimate partner violence.

He Loses Control

One of the most common excuses for domestic violence is that the offender, normally a good guy, simply loses control, which results in violence and abuse. There are various specific explanations for this loss of control, such as the offender being excessively angry and in need of anger management training, or simply having a violent, explosive personality, but the underlying assumption in all of these excuses is that the violence took place in a fit of emotion that the man had no control over. Let's take a closer look at that assumption.

First, it plays on stereotypes of abusive men as lower class, muscle-bound atavists. This stereotype is not true, as upper class men who are professionals have the potential to abuse, as well. While intimate partner violence is *reported* more often in the lower classes, there are a number of good reasons to suspect that reporting differences might be manifestations of lower class life more so than actual differences in rates. For example, poorer people more often live in apartments or smaller, cheaper homes that are built more closely together. In both instances, the sound of an altercation is more likely to be heard—and reported—to the police than for people living in homes with better sound-proofing and more distance from neighbors.

Further, the common characterization of domestic violence as a lower class phenomenon likely increases the embarrassment and shame associated with reporting for middle and upper class victims. Domestic violence simply isn't supposed to happen to them, so experiencing it probably feels especially surreal and shameful, leading to less reporting. Finally, victims with more financial resources may be able to get out of the situation more quietly and easily than victims who have less. Their families and friends are likely to be in a better position to help, and the offender may not resort to violent retaliation in public as often in order to save face in the community. There are notable exceptions to this, of course, but for the most part, we see more reporting in the lower classes, but we are far from certain that this really equates to less offending in the middle and upper classes.

Offenders do not necessarily fit the stereotype of the blue-collar tough guy. Many are quite gentle and sweet to everyone else. They can be charming, calm and reasonable. They tend to talk a lot about their feelings, in part because their feelings are so important to them relative to the feelings of their partner. College-educated offenders are often particularly adept at confusing and undermining their victims verbally, and at convincing other people that the victim is crazy (or abusive, or awful, etc.). Perpetrators with economic and social power are in a position to offend with near impunity, as their resources make it difficult for others to believe that they are offenders due to the low-class stereotype. Overall, the idea that men lose control is firmly entrenched in the idea that intimate partner violence is something blue collar and unemployed toughs do—men who lack control over their behavior. Nothing could be further from the truth.

Another problem with the loss of control/anger excuse is that a closer look at situations in which offenders "lose control" often reveals interesting patterns that suggest otherwise. Perhaps he is going crazy and breaking things around the house in a threatening manner because he's just "lost it," but a quick inventory of the broken items often reveals that the victim's possessions were targeted—not the offender's. This suggests an obvious element of control. Similarly, perpetrators often limit themselves in other ways, such as not hurting a victim to the extent that she will require medical treatment, stopping abuse before it gets loud enough to draw police attention, only abusing the victim when outsiders are not there to witness it, or suddenly turning into a very nice, rational guy the moment the police arrive.[18]

Perpetrators are all about control, and are making a choice to let themselves go when they offend because it suits their needs. It is very frightening when someone looks out-of-control in a state of anger, and it is a quick and effective way to cow someone when less dramatic tactics fail. Offenders have a host of excuses for why they abuse; it is rare to hear them say "I don't know" in response to questions about why they did it, but that is exactly the answer you would expect from someone who had genuinely lost control over themselves. Abusers give themselves permission to turn themselves loose, but even then, they are not truly out-of-control.

He's Mentally Ill

The last category in this discussion is mental illness, and it is an important topic to address because so many people believe that perpetrators are mentally ill in the aftermath of violence that comes to public attention. When an offender kills or seriously injures his partner or children, it is easy to think that they must be crazy. They look mentally ill, after all: They seem irrational to the victim when they accuse her of having affairs with unlikely people, explode over a dinner that is not cooked to their specifications or go nuts when the house is not just as they like it. However, more often than not, people outside of the relationship do not see the offender as mentally ill, unless and until he commits public violence.

In fact, the vast majority of offenders are not mentally ill; crazy behavior just works well for them as both an effective tactic and built-in excuse. Very serious offenders do have an increased likelihood of mental illness, but there is not a typical diagnosis that they share. In other words, the mental illness is not driving the abuse. Emotional disturbances do not cause abuse any more than alcohol or drugs do, they simply interact with the abusiveness to form a volatile combination of violent factors. Millions of people suffer from psychiatric disorders but do not perpetrate violence against their intimate partners.

Excuses from offenders are not difficult to understand. They are designed to deflect the fault for the violence away from the offender, and are common to all crime types, not just intimate partner violence. What is interesting is the extent to which these excuses have been appropriated as causes for domestic violence at a societal level. Generally, we do not put much stock in the excuses of burglars, robbers and murderers, but for some reason, people look for justifications for perpetrators of intimate partner violence. Given that rape is about the only other offense for which we do this, it is difficult to escape the conclusion that we only tend to excuse offenders in the case of violence perpetrated largely against women. Lundy Bancroft points out that he has never had a client who said, "There's no way to defend what I did. It was just totally wrong."[19] Offenders nearly always make excuses for their behavior. What is important is to step back and see those justifications for what they are.

Variations in Types of Perpetrators

Perpetrators of intimate partner violence vary greatly from offender to offender on a number of measures, but we thought it is important to try to give at least a brief typology to illustrate the kinds of violence and control you might encounter in your everyday life or career because it is so important to classify risk correctly. This is not to say that an offender who is only exhibiting lower-level abuse might not suddenly escalate, or that a serious offender might not—only that the likelihood of some offenders becoming seriously violent is greater, and particularly where resources need to be carefully allocated due to scarcity, it is important to know these distinctions.

There are some behaviors and attitudes common to all perpetrators, whether they are simply controlling and manipulative in an abusive way, or frequently physically violent. One common feature that is important for professionals to be aware of is a victim mentality. When you respond to intimate partner violence, it is incredibly likely that the offender will try to turn the situation around to present himself as the victim. He might report that his partner is crazy, and present himself as the beleaguered partner trying to deal with her mental illness. He might point to defensive wounds to claim that he is the abused partner, and only resorted to violence to protect himself. The victim is likely to be out-of-sorts, making it easier for the perpetrator to cast her as dramatic, crazy, vindictive or a liar. As a professional responding to these crimes, it is very important to be aware of this phenomenon, because perpetrators really do feel put-upon, and thus can be quite convincing to the uninitiated. The offender convinces the victim that her behavior is responsible for his violence more easily because the offender really believes it is her fault, in part to alleviate any guilt he might feel for hurting her.[20]

Jealousy is another common feature in offenders, though this is not limited to sexual jealousy. This jealousy stems from a pervasive sense of entitlement on the part of the perpetrator, which causes him to expect to come before everything and everyone else in the victim's life. Children, jobs, friendships, hobbies, even a commute—all are activities that can elicit morbid jealousy, because they take the victim away from what the offender views as her primary responsibility: attending to his needs and desires.

This sense of entitlement is an almost standard feature in perpetrators of all stripes, and it is responsible for both the jealousy and the ideation that the perpetrator is actually the victim, as women are unable to live up to the constantly escalating expectations of the offender. They are bottomless pits when it comes to their partners, and eventually, no matter how hard she tries, he will be dissatisfied and resort to abuse or battering in an effort to control her to better attend to his desires. Certainly sexual jealousy is a regular feature in many abusive relationships, as well, but these other types of jealousy are often overlooked.

There are a plethora of tactics and patterns common to intimate violence perpetrators, so the following typology should by no means be considered exhaustive. Moreover, perpetrators do not always fit neatly into one category, and might shift categories on a regular basis. All violence is serious, but when tactics start to escalate without regard to legal or social consequences, it is another sign that the offender is getting into more dangerous territory with his abuse and violence. This is part of why even the lowest-level abuse is of concern, aside from its harmful effect on the victim, despite not reaching the threshold of a criminal designation. Many women who are killed by their perpetrators do not have a single bruise on them—the tactics are fluid and escalate.

Abusive Tactics

Perpetrators using abusive tactics mentally abuse, manipulate and otherwise control their partners. They use subtle threats and suggestions of violence, as well as physically intimidating behavior, such as throwing things, using their size and proximity, and "playing" with weapons to instill fear. They usually maintain their public image as respectable and non-abusive. This makes it that much more difficult to have those on the outside of the relationship see him the way she does. He knows this and cultivates a "but he's such a nice guy!" image. Here, perpetrators use subtler tactics like intimidation, coercion, threats and isolation with their victims before they escalate to physical violence. They are (usually) not arrested for these offenses, but they successfully traumatize and confuse victims within the relationship. Perpetrators using these tactics rarely do anything for which they might be arrested, while wreaking havoc covertly. They have an engrained sense of entitlement in their relationship with intimates, and expect them to act according to their wishes and demands. Society still reinforces the notion of male supremacy and superiority in a variety of ways, mainly through our laws and in the media, which exacerbates this sense of entitlement.

Perpetrators are at risk for engaging battering and terroristic tactics if they lose control of their victim, but may never escalate to a stage of physical dangerousness. The problem for victims is that it is very difficult to tell if the offender will escalate to physical violence, or allow them to leave the relationship. Perpetrators are ready, willing and able to escalate their controlling tactics to include physical attacks at any point in time, but they usually resort to physical abuse when they feel the other tactics are not working sufficiently. Victims deserve and need (or at least benefit greatly from) support and intervention from their local domestic violence program, as well as acceptance and support from family and friends. Advocates can assist the victim with safety planning and lethality assessments. Both are vitally important as she contemplates separating from him, as this is the most dangerous time for her, the children, her family and the public. The case of Marlene illustrates a few abusive tactics that are not uncommon, but the varieties are almost endless.

Marlene was married to a successful businessman. During their courtship and into the beginning of their marriage, he was charming and seemed to be a devoted husband. Several years into the marriage, when Marlene got pregnant, her husband became tense, agitated and withdrawn. They had had numerous discussions about having children and he said he wanted children soon, but once Marlene was actually pregnant, her husband became increasingly hostile, controlling and demanding, and seemed to resent her being pregnant. He expected her to do "the smallest things" like stay on the phone for only 2 minutes. He would put an egg timer beside the phone when she started to talk with her mother or a friend, and she was expected to be off the phone by the time the sand had run through to the bottom. He also created rules about when to use the air conditioner and at which temperature she was "allowed" to set the air conditioner. Another "rule" he established for her was the proper way to "use the toilet." His "rules" included when she was allowed and not allowed to flush the toilet.

Marlene was ashamed of the rules her husband established for her, but they were married in the 1960s and they were Jewish, so she believed she was expected to do the "best she could" with the situation for both her family and her faith. As time went by, the rules became even more numerous and punitive, and Marlene felt infantilized by her husband. Finally, when she could no longer take him running her life as he did, she took her son and left. She had to endure judgment from many in her community, and for years she felt as if she had "failed," but she wanted a better, less restrictive and fearful life for herself and her son.

It wasn't easy, especially in the days before the battered women's movement started to provide women like Marlene with access to support and resources and a sense of community, but looking back on everything now, Marlene knows she did the right thing. Her son grew up in a home where he felt safe and loved, and not afraid to make mistakes. He still maintained a relationship with his father, but he was able to learn from his mother that women deserved to be treated with the kind of respect she never got. Her son is now in a loving and respectful marriage, and Marlene, who now knows that there is much more to abuse than physical violence, works with survivors of domestic violence.

The crux of abusive tactics is control. In a sense, the perpetrator is training his victim to take orders from him, and this can range from subtle "suggestions" (you look better when you wear dresses) to rules (you will always call or text when you go anywhere beyond work), to commands backed by threats of physical violence (do this or you are going to make me angry, and that isn't good for you). These tactics all serve to increase the perpetrator's control over the victim until living in this state of control feels normal.

Battering Tactics

Battering tactics are employed to mentally and physically abuse, manipulate and otherwise control a perpetrator's partner. Offenders may periodically use violence in the form of beating or otherwise harming the victim without a weapon, along with physical and verbal intimidation. Battering perpetrators engage in violence for which they would be eligible for arrest, but still put energy into maintaining a public façade of respectability. They are good at manipulating potential allies and police into believing the victim is exaggerating the violence, or is otherwise lying about the violent situation. They are more likely to escalate to terrorism in the event that the victim is able to extricate herself from the relationship. The victim will likely require domestic violence services, such as a shelter and advocacy, in order to safely leave the relationship. The case of Susan illustrates the move from abusive to battering tactics.

To nearly everyone on the outside, Susan looked like everything in her life was perfect. She was bright and beautiful, had three wonderful kids and a good job. But behind closed doors, she also had a husband who was verbally, emotionally and physically abusive to her. He seemed to take particular delight in using harsh language and intimidation to diminish her as much as possible. It did not matter what Susan tried: He always found a reason to abuse her.

During one particularly ugly assault, her husband demanded that their 13-year-old son get a video camera and turn it on Susan as he threatened and belittled her. He was so intimidating that he got his son to join in abusing Susan. While his son continued to run the video camera, Susan's husband physically assaulted her over and over again.

Susan knew that she had to get away, but she also knew what her husband was capable of, so it took careful planning for her to take the kids and break free. One of the things Susan was not aware of was the fact that her friend and office mate was secretly making notes on her desk calendar every time Susan showed up at work with bruises on her face, or whenever she heard her on the phone with him. Often, he made her refer to him as "master." It was a brutal existence.

When the day came for Susan to leave, her friend helped her. They needed to act quickly because Susan had a very limited amount of time to get the kids and contact the police. When she did go to the police, the detective suggested she call her husband and tell him she was not coming back. He made more threats against Susan and the phone call was recorded.

He was arrested and charged with misdemeanor domestic violence based on the videotape that had been made. But he was only charged with a single count. As much as the detectives and the prosecutor wanted to charge him with more, they said the assault that was recorded was "just one assault" despite the fact that it had gone on for close to an hour. But then the detectives spoke with Susan's friend and office mate. She showed them her desk calendar. She had documented 36 separate assaults, so Susan's husband was charged with 36 misdemeanors. When he was tried and found guilty, he was sentenced to 36 years, the longest sentence ever given in the state of New York for misdemeanor crimes.

Susan has come a long way since she freed herself from her perpetrator.

Terroristic Tactics

Terroristic tactics are employed to mentally and physically abuse, manipulate and otherwise control partners just as with abusive and battering strategies, but they also incorporate the threat of or use of weapons in the violence. Offenders keep an even tighter rein on their victims through fear, coercion and violence. Terrorists threaten to kill the victim, her children or other loved ones if they ever leave or somehow cross the offender. They are still able to maintain a façade of respectability, but may care less about doing so as victims are so cowed that there is less cause to defend themselves to outsiders. They may be less adept at manipulating law enforcement due to the seriousness of the crimes they commit, and their deep-seated belief that they have the right to commit the offenses against their victims.

Terrorists are less amenable to legal remedies, often engaging in a host of illegal activities toward the victim, such as stalking, threatening with a weapon, assault and destruction of property. They are more likely than other types of perpetrators to engage in violence and other criminal activity outside of the home, and are more likely to use a gun against the victim. There is an increased risk of murder-suicide and mass shootings with this type of offender, and the victim is at far greater risk for serious violence if she leaves. The victim will require extensive assistance to leave the relationship, and protection for a longer period in the wake of leaving in order to stay safe.

On January 16, 2014, Lindon, Utah police officer Joshua Boren failed to report to work for his shift. Police went to do a well-being check and made a gruesome discovery. Inside the house, they found the bodies of Kelly Boren, Joshua's wife, their two children, 7-year-old Joshua (Jaden) and 5-year-old Haley and 55-year-old

Marie King, Kelly Boren's mother. They had all been shot and killed. Joshua Boren had turned the gun on himself after he killed his family. He used his service weapon.

His fellow officers and police administrators were stunned. Boren had been in law enforcement for over 7 years, first as a deputy sheriff and then as a patrol officer. He was described by his colleagues as a great cop, a cop's cop and a great dad, but an investigation conducted by the Spanish Fork Police Department uncovered a much darker and disturbed Joshua Boren, someone who, when he felt his cover was going to be blown and was going to lose his family, committed a horrendous act of domestic terrorism.

Despite his friendly outward demeanor, he had been drugging and sexually assaulting his wife, and videotaping these assaults. Kelly discovered the tapes in 2013 and shared the information with a few friends, but she did not go to the police because she did not want his career to be compromised. She did, however, tell Joshua that she was going to leave and take the children. The night before the homicides took place, she texted Joshua and told him, "I hate my life because of you. You killed a part of me." She also texted, "I don't want to live in fear and hate and anger" and used the word "rape" when she was communicating with him. He texted her back saying, "Don't involve the kids. They are innocent."

Joshua's therapist disclosed that he had been sexually abused as a boy, that he had a pornography addiction, that his father had committed suicide when he was 5, and that he despised his mother. And yet he was able to keep these aspects of his life hidden from everyone at the sheriff and police departments.

Abusers often work very hard at controlling their public personas. This makes it especially hard for the victims to be taken seriously when they ask for help. The issue with dual personalities is compounded when the abuser is someone held in high esteem, such as a law enforcement officer, a pastor, a doctor or a bank president. It is extremely difficult to reconcile the two personalities, and as a result, victims are even more reluctant to disclose what is happening behind closed doors. The perpetrator knows this and it emboldens him. At the same time, the victim feels diminished not only through his abuse, but also by the social trap she knows she is caught in.

We think we have a sense, based on the 9/11 attacks and other acts of terrorism that are both religiously and culturally motivated, of what a terrorist looks like. But what happens if the terrorist is our next-door neighbor, the guy who helped fix a fence or change a tire? The very nature of domestic violence is that it takes place behind closed doors, out of the gaze of a condemning public. While there are some perpetrators who care little about what the public thinks of them (gang members, bikers, etc.), many of the most dangerous domestic terrorists are the ones we would never suspect as being capable of annihilating their entire family, like Officer Joshua Boren. We are collectively stunned by these tragedies that are viewed as rare, shocking events—but that happen with alarming frequency.

Risk Factors versus Causation

In Chapter 4, we will explore factors that are correlated with intimate partner violence, but the material in the current chapter warrants a quick note about risk factors and causation. Because domestic violence has such a long history of being excused and justified, it is especially important to take care to avoid confusing factors associated with an increased risk for intimate partner violence with *causes* of intimate partner violence. As in the case of rape, where a short skirt or high level of blood alcohol are not the cause of the crime, in domestic violence, fighting back or ending up in a relationship with a perpetrator in the first place does not justify the offense, either.

Similarly, the fact that more people are arrested for intimate partner violence from the lower classes does not mean that anything about being lower class causes domestic violence, or that domestic violence does not take place in middle and upper class families (and probably at a much higher rate than we know about, as noted earlier). If a man routinely uses his size or demeanor to intimidate other people, then it is very likely that his intimate partner will end up at the wrong end of his intimidation tactics at some point. Intimidating behavior is a risk factor for intimate partner violence, but it is very important to remember that it is not the cause of it—it is far from necessary for a man to be intimidating to others to abuse his intimate partner.

Criminology deals in generalizations; risk factors are important, and can help victims protect themselves from violence, but they are not sufficient in and of themselves to cause the crime to occur. Always remember: The offender is the cause of intimate partner violence.

In Chapter 3, we will discuss the specific issues and difficulties in leaving a violent intimate partner relationship. All of the means of control you have just read about come into play in a victim attempting to leave her abuser, and more. While most people think that leaving is a no-brainer, it is an extremely difficult and dangerous thing for a victim to do.

What You Can Do

- Be alert for signs of covert control in domestic violence situations. A "look" can be enough to control a victim in the presence of police or others (think about the power many mothers have to curb bad behavior with a pointed look at children, and then add the threat of real violence to the mix).
- Ask victims to describe their everyday situations with the offender. Encourage them to acknowledge and talk about the nonviolent control in their relationships and take it seriously as an indication of danger. A question that will help get the victim to start opening up is to simply ask "Does he control you in your daily life? Are there things you cannot do because he doesn't want you to do them?"
- Tell victims you are afraid for their safety (and the safety of her children if she has any) and that you are there for them. Having someone explicitly express concern is both comforting and reinforcing. It is telling the victim you believe her, and that you believe her interpretation of the perpetrator's actions.
- Always remember that victims are the experts on their situations and their perpetrator. If the victim says something is threatening, it's threatening, whether it seems threatening to you or not. Remember that perpetrators often use tactics that seem nonthreatening on their face intentionally—they only escalate to more violent and unambiguous threats if they need to in order to maintain or regain control.

- Recognize that violence is only one tool of many used to maintain control over victims. Other types of control are damaging and should be treated as significant (especially as they are often indicative of future physical violence). See Appendix I for examples of these tactics.
- It is useful to have a copy of the Power and Control Wheel available for the victim to review. Many victims do not recognize the nonphysical forms of abuse as dangerous. It helps when they see it and are able to identify the things the abuser does that are unique to their relationship.
- Help the victim understand how common intimate partner violence is. Breaking down her sense of isolation is an important first step.
- Help intimate partner violence victims regain their sense of self through explaining that the negative messages they received about themselves were a method of control on the part of the offender.
- Use the Lethality Assessment Program (LAP) (Appendix II) tool to aid you in determining risk, but remember that it is just a guide. Use your gut instinct, as well. LAP is as much an art as a science.
- Access to firearms significantly increases lethality risks for the victim/s and for law enforcement. Find out how many firearms he has and how he uses them to threaten her.
- Be especially vigilant and proactive in intimate partner violence situations in which the offender has threatened the life of the victim or those she loves.
- Ask her if she has ever tried to leave before, and if so, what happened. Has he ever threatened to hurt or kill her when/if she leaves?
- Find out if he has ever strangled her before, or threatened to. Strangulation assaults are another high-risk indicator.
- Always try to help connect intimate partner violence victims with resources such as advocates, help lines or shelters. It may take a while for such contact to result in a woman being able to leave, but it is essential to begin countering the negative, inaccurate messages the victim is receiving in the relationship.

Discussion Ideas

1. List every reason (or excuse) for intimate partner violence that you have ever heard.[21] Try to organize them into three categories: myths, partial truths and accurate statements. Discuss.
2. Which excuses for intimate partner violence have you believed in the past? Why?
3. Discuss why intimate partner violence is treated and viewed so differently than other types of crime.
4. Discuss types of coercion and control you have seen or experienced at work in relationships.
5. Is the word "abuse" a problem? Is it overused or trivialized? How about the term "domestic violence"?
6. Should crimes of domestic violence be considered hate crimes because they're gender specific (with very rare exceptions)?

References and Notes

1. To learn even more about this sort of control, we highly recommend E. Stark, *Coercive Control: How Men Entrap Women in Personal Life* (New York: Oxford University Press, 2007). See also, I. Marcus, Reframing 'Domestic Violence': Terrorism in the home, in *The Public Nature of Private Violence: The Discovery of Domestic Abuse*, eds. M. Fineman and R. Mykitiuk (New York: Routledge, 1994), 11–35.
2. Though an in-depth discussion is beyond the scope of this book, animal abuse is frequently used as a tactic to control and terrorize victims. For an overview, see V. Upadhya, The abuse of animals as a method of domestic violence: The need for criminalization, *Emory Law Journal* 63; 2014: 1163–209.
3. Also see Appendix III; L. K. Bledsoe and B. K. Sar, Intimate partner violence control scale: Development and initial testing, *Journal of Family Violence* 26; 2011: 171–84.
4. L. Bancroft, *Why Does He Do That? Inside the Minds of Angry and Controlling Men* (New York: Berkley Books, 2003).
5. L. E. Walker, *The Battered Woman Syndrome*, 3rd ed. (New York: Springer, 2009).
6. L. Chamberlain and R. Levenson, *Addressing Intimate Partner Violence, Reproductive and Sexual Coercion: A Guide for Obstetric, Gynecologic and Reproductive Health Care Settings*, 2nd ed. (San Francisco, CA: Futures without Violence, 2012).
7. See Appendix I.

8. A. Biblarz, J. T. Barnowe, and D. Biblarz, To tell or not to tell: Differences between victims who report crimes and victims who do not, *Victimology* 9; 1984: 153–8.
9. O. W. Barnett, C. L. Miller-Perrin, and R. D. Perrin, *Family Violence across the Lifespan,* 2nd ed. (Thousand Oaks, CA: Sage, 2005); A. Chornesky, The dynamics of battering revisited, *Journal of Women and Social Work* 15; 2000: 480–501, http://citeseerx.ist.psu.edu/viewdoc/download?doi=10.1.1.122.9414&rep=rep1&type=pdf (accessed March 12, 2015).
10. American Psychological Association, *Violence and the Family* (Washington, DC: Presidential Task Force on Violence and the Family, 1996).
11. This idea was posited in S. Forward, *Men Who Hate Women and the Women Who Love Them* (New York: Bantam Books, 2002).
12. L. Bancroft, *Why Does He Do That? Inside the Minds of Angry and Controlling Men* (New York: Berkley Books, 2003). We are deeply indebted to Lundy Bancroft and his experience counseling batterers for helping to inform this section of the book.
13. Ibid.
14. Ibid.
15. Ibid.
16. Ibid.
17. Ibid.
18. Ironically, this often makes the victim, who is very upset and frightened, look crazy and out-of-control by comparison.
19. Ibid.
20. We will discuss the impact of this phenomenon on perceptions about male victims in Chapter 4.
21. L. Bancroft, *Why Does He Do That? Inside the Minds of Angry and Controlling Men* (New York: Berkley Books, 2003).

3
The Truth About Leaving

One of the most troubling aspects of intimate partner violence for people on the outside of abusive relationships is why women do not just leave the situation. There are a variety of extremely good reasons why victims do not leave, but chief among them is that it is the most dangerous point for women in domestic violence situations in terms of homicide risk.[1] It is a wrenching catch-22: Estimates show that victims are 75% more likely to be murdered when they try to leave or have left than when they stay.[2] Many victims of intimate partner violence sense this intuitively even where they are unaware of the statistics. For many, the question itself is fuelled by underlying beliefs that women remaining in the violent relationship must be codependent, stupid or masochistic.[3] Nothing could be further from the truth. There are a myriad of reasons why women stay in a violent relationship, or make several attempts to leave before getting out permanently, none of which have anything to do with codependency, stupidity or masochism.

Navigating the legal, social and familial issues necessary to leave can be overwhelming enough without the threat of serious violence or death that often accompanies even the consideration of getting out. It is easy for victims, who are already compromised by the perpetrators emotionally and often physically, to become discouraged, intimidated and hopeless over the prospect of overcoming all the necessary hurdles.[4] When people assume that women simply have to leave to end the violence, they betray a lack of understanding about how intimate partner violence manifests itself.

A woman leaving a violent relationship represents a complete loss of control on the part of the offender, so it is not surprising that violence often escalates as he attempts to regain his power over her. Perpetrators feel a sense of entitlement with respect to their partners, and leaving is the ultimate rebuke of this notion. Women are frequently threatened with homicide if they ever leave, and given the number of murders committed by estranged intimate partners, this threat is credible. Worse, offenders often threaten children, loved ones and even pets with injury or death in order to keep a woman from even contemplating leaving.[5]

Reasons Women Stay in Abusive Relationships

It is easy for an estranged intimate partner to stalk his victim—after all, he knows where she works, shops, where her family lives, where her children go to school—and children often necessitate contact legally.[6] Fear of retaliation is *very* rational on the part of victims, not an overreaction or dramatic ideation, despite the fact that few people can believe that lethal violence is likely to occur (prior to the lethal event—in retrospect, it often appears to have been inevitable). When well-meaning outsiders, including law enforcement and social workers, push women to leave, they often minimize the risk of serious physical assault or death at the victim's peril.

There are a variety of reasons why a woman might feel she cannot leave a violent relationship beyond fear, and financial concerns are chief among them. Money is too often the reason why women do not leave, or why they go back after leaving. Especially where children are involved, it is common to find that a woman cannot provide for her family without the assistance of the perpetrator. These days, few families can afford to exist on one salary. A study in Texas found that 85% of victims who called shelters, hotlines and emergency rooms had left their partners no less than five times, and that the number one reason victims gave for going back to the offender was financial.[7]

Temporary Assistance for Needy Families (TANF) is the primary safety net for most victims trying to leave their abuser, and it provides so little support that even with that assistance, many women are unable to feed and shelter their families. For 99% of those receiving TANF benefits, the purchasing power of the assistance they receive is below 1996 levels adjusting for inflation, and even when victims qualify for and receive Supplemental Nutrition Assistance Program (SNAP) benefits in addition to TANF, they still fall below the poverty line.[8] Further, navigating the process to apply and qualify for such assistance is onerous, working is difficult due to childcare costs, the need to remain eligible for benefits makes working a tightrope act, working brings with it the fear of being tracked down by the perpetrator, and, in many cases, the physical and psychological state of the victim contributes to financial difficulties.

Of course, there are a host of other reasons why women stay aside from the need to support children. Victims might believe it is in the children's best interests to have two parents if the perpetrator does not beat the children, without being aware of the harmful impact of witnessing violence in the home even where child abuse is not occurring simultaneously.[9] Children might also exert pressure on the victim to stay, especially in response to manipulation on the part of the offender, which is not uncommon.[10]

An example of this kind of manipulation involved a woman in North Carolina who was married to an alcoholic who worked only when he felt like it. They had five children. At one point, he beat her so badly that she had to be hospitalized with a broken jaw. Just before Christmas and a few days before she was scheduled to be released, the hospital social worker called a local advocate to help the woman get an Order of Protection. Her jaw was wired shut so she had to write the answers to the advocate's questions. The woman's husband was at the hearing and stood up to tell the judge that he "had nowhere to go."

The judge ordered him out of the house and set the next hearing for the first week of the new year. At the 10-day hearing, the advocate met with the victim in the courthouse. Her jaw was still wired shut, and she could not make eye contact with the advocate. When the advocate asked her how she was, she wrote on a piece of paper that her out-of-work husband showed up at the house on Christmas morning with an armload of presents for the children. Naturally, they were thrilled to see him. He was sober and "the perfect dad" during the visit. When it came time for him to go, he reached for the front door handle, looked back at the children, and said, "I'd love to be here but your Mother won't let me," and then walked out.

The children turned to her and begged, repeatedly, "We want daddy back." Never mind that he had broken her jaw: The kids wanted their (sober) daddy back and she felt she would disappoint the children if she said no, so she wanted to withdraw the Order of Protection. It wasn't because she was no longer afraid of him; she simply knew that the consequences of saying no would be to upset the children.

Fear of losing children to the perpetrator in a child custody battle can also thwart attempts to escape violence.[11] Threats regarding custody are a common ploy used by offenders to keep women from leaving, and in a significant number of cases, men are successful in garnering some form of custody from the courts,[12] which ties the victim to the perpetrator indefinitely with the added terror of having to turn her children over to him periodically. The woman might even feel grateful to the abuser for helping to raise and support her children, particularly if they are from a previous relationship.[13]

We would be remiss if we failed to mention the role of hope in keeping women in violent relationships. Attorney, domestic violence advocate and intimate partner violence survivor, Sarah Buel offers this on the topic of hope in preventing women from leaving their abusers:

> A victim's hope for the violence to cease is typically fueled by the batterer's promises to change; pleas from the children; clergy members' admonishments to pray more; the family's advice to save the relationship; and other well-intentioned, but dangerously misguided counsel. Many victims are hopeful because they want so desperately to believe that *this* time the batterer really has seen the error of his ways and intends to change, not realizing that, without serious interventions, chances are slim that the abuse will stop.[14]

Add this to the isolation and low self-esteem that victims regularly experience in violent intimate partnerships, and it is not surprising that many women hang on, hoping that the situation will get better and the violence will end.

Typically, the woman is in love with the perpetrator, as well. Love is complicated, and we do not always reserve our love for people who deserve it. Before judging, it might be worth recalling friendships and colleagues in which you may have forgiven or overlooked bad behavior, hanging on in the hope that earlier feelings in the relationship would be restored. Intimate partnerships are our primary relationships, and thus we tend to work harder to keep them intact. Add to this that domestic violence victims are isolated from other relationships that might offer support and comfort, and you can see where love and hope can significantly impact someone's desire for it to work out.

Finally, victims are sometimes embarrassed to find themselves in this sort of predicament, and fear being judged if they "come out" as being abused. Fear of judgment is a key feature in underreporting to the police and others, and embarrassment likely exacerbates underreporting, particularly in the case of victims from higher-class homes, as they might have associations with domestic violence as being a lower-class phenomenon. Victims risk not being believed, having the problem minimized, pressure to leave when they are not ready or too frightened, and being blamed for the violence, among other possibilities. Black women frequently experience the added burden of displeasure from others if she reports the violence to law enforcement due to cultural pressures against "getting" another black man arrested and possibly incarcerated.[15] In this manner, black victims report, "being forced to choose between gender and race in deciding whether to use the criminal justice system for relief."[16]

This list is far from exhaustive, but should give you a better idea of the factors that contribute to women's reluctance to leave an abusive relationship. Remember, though, that fear and financial limitations are chief among these reasons.

People outside of the domestic violence community often do not think past the woman getting out of the house or relationship, but that is frequently when the real terrorism begins. Intimate partner violence rarely features easy answers, and even where women are able to leave, extracting themselves from the relationship is no panacea for the violence and control. Obviously, leaving the perpetrator is a crucial step toward ending the violence, but it is not the last step, and it is anything but an easy step.

The Myth of the Perfect Victim

For many of us, our sense of what it means to be a crime victim comes from the media. Whether it's an episode of *CSI* or *Law and Order*, or a crime "reality" show like *48 Hours*, *20/20*, or *Dateline*, the entire process seems to move along at a fairly reliable pace, and the participants assume reliable roles. The defendants have all kinds of excuses for what has happened (cue the victim-blaming), and the victims (or their surviving family members) are most often innocent people in the wrong place at the wrong time. In reality, victims are rarely so perfect. They have problems like everyone else, make bad decisions, simply lack knowledge that places them in harm's way, might be involved in illegal activity themselves, and generally don't resemble victims on television. For many reasons, victims of intimate partner violence are especially likely to look far from perfect, and it is important for law enforcement and other potential support people to recognize this and alter their expectations. Nobody deserves to be assaulted or live in fear, and it is important to remember that many of the qualities that inspire less sympathy—indecision, lethargy, drug or alcohol use and the like—are actually symptoms of the intimate partner victimization that they've endured.

When the crimes are "domestic" in nature, all bets as to how the victim will behave go out the window. One of the most frustrating characteristics of domestic violence victims is that they are so often unwilling or unable to leave the perpetrator. To outsiders, this seems inconceivable and suspect. If the woman is being assaulted, it seems obvious that the solution is to leave immediately. This is why it is so important to remember that leaving is a process, not an event, and that, for most victims, that process comes in fits and starts. When you step back and look at how difficult and scary leaving is from the victim's standpoint, the situation makes far more sense, and the victim seems far less messy. It may take her a period of time before she even begins to recognize that the dynamics of her relationship have become dangerous. Moreover, even as she comes to this realization, he will be actively working against her, employing the tactics we have discussed to keep her isolated and confused. Add fear to that mix, and it's easy to see how her options seem about as clear as mud. Add concerns about money, children, retaliation, the reactions of friends and family, and a host of other worries, and it is far easier to understand why victims don't just leave. It is crucial that you don't blame her for her being unable to extricate herself from her predicament.

An accepted statistic about domestic violence holds that it takes the average victim leaving five to seven times before she leaves for good.

The way this usually works out is that the first one to three times, she flees without any advance planning, usually with the clothes on her back and her children. She might go to a shelter for abused women, or she may go to stay with family or friends, but wherever she goes, the abuser immediately begins the process of doing whatever he can to lure her back. It might be promises ("I'll never do it again," "I'll start going to church," or "You knew that would piss me off and you still did it."). He may return to the "really nice guy" persona to convince her that the abuse was just aberrant behavior. He may turn on the charm with her friends and family to enlist them in helping to coerce her into coming home. Alternatively, he may go to their pastor, rabbi or imam and get them to "help" her see that she just needs to come home and be a better wife or girlfriend. The external sources of pressure are legion, and soon she feels overwhelmed and returns to her abuser. Add to that the sad truth that staying at a shelter is something akin to willingly putting yourself in a refugee camp, no matter how nice the accommodations or staff, and the cards are stacked in the perpetrator's favor.

Often, when she fails to leave, she's doing precisely what everyone has told her to do: "Give him another chance—he probably didn't mean to do it," or "He seems like a nice guy to me." Then, when the abuse starts again, she feels responsible and that she's let others down as well as her partner, and the self-isolation begins as she doesn't want to admit that it's happening again. This is precisely what he wants; the more isolated she is, the more control he has over her. The downward spiral gains both momentum and significance. This scenario is good for the perpetrator, and very bad for the victim, who will need to summon even more resolve to leave again given this experience.

Often times, victims' lives are complex in ways that both transcend and intersect the current instance of intimate violence. Some may have been sexually abused as children, or exposed to domestic violence as they grew up, making abusive interpersonal dynamics seem normal to them. Some have turned to drugs or alcohol to self-medicate. Many are profoundly depressed or suffer from anxiety. These and other issues make it very likely that she will face judgment when she reaches out for help, and she is aware of that.

The victim's use of drugs and/or alcohol can be an excuse the perpetrator uses to justify his actions. For example, in Durham, North

Carolina a number of years ago, a young black woman came home high on crack cocaine. Her boyfriend became enraged with her and strangled her to death. The district attorney determined that he was not guilty of murder in that he was justified in killing her because of her drugged state. He was sentenced to 90 days in the Durham County jail. This is not an isolated event.

When advocates work with abused women, they understand that victims sometimes turn to drugs or alcohol as a way to cope with their situation. Further, these victims often have multiple layers of issues to be addressed, and they tend to dovetail into each other. They can seem hostile and mistrustful, but good advocates recognize that they should be feeling that way, and give them both the space and support to start to talk it through. Building a trusting relationship with someone who has been routinely abused, frightened, diminished and marginalized takes time, but it is vital to the victim's healing process.

Victims may have had interactions with many people who hold them responsible for the perpetrator's choice to be abusive, controlling and violent. It's a heavy load to carry for the victim, and those attitudes allow him to continue his abuse. Law enforcement officers respond to a 911 call and he seems cool, calm and collected, while she's crying and agitated, making the officers feel uncomfortable in her presence. This feeds directly into the narrative that the perpetrator is crafting, making the victim look out-of-control, rather than the offender. If he is compliant with the police, when the case goes to trial, the investigating officers will be called as witnesses *for him*, and they will testify to his calm demeanor on the scene. On the other hand, the victim is more likely to be described in the police report as "hysterical," "demanding," or the worst thing a woman can possibly be: angry.

Some abuse victims have complex mental health issues, but many are simply depressed because they are being abused. If the victim has a diagnosed mental health issue, abusers can use that against her as well. The perpetrator may know that she will not be able to take the witness stand, so he can do whatever he wants to her. I once worked with a woman with a severe bipolar disorder that was exacerbated by her husband's abuse and his alcoholism. The neighbors would call the police when they heard him beating her up, but when the police arrived, he would tell them that she was in a manic state and he was simply trying to calm her down. She would come to our agency and talk about the things that were happening, and how hard it was for her to "keep it together." We understood what she was up against: an abusive, alcoholic husband, bipolar disorder and four kids to care for. She was not a perfect victim, but she was a victim nonetheless, and she deserved our help and support. Sometimes, she would just come to the agency to go into a quiet room and take a nap. That was what she needed in the moment, so we provided it for her. It is not our job to determine how a victim should be acting or responding to what is happening to her: It is our job to be there for her wherever she is at that point, and to support her in a nonjudgmental manner.

By the time victims have left their perpetrators several times and the cycle does not end, they begin to see that his behavior does not hinge on her. It's simply about his choice to abuse and control her. Blaming her or other issues is just an excuse. Early attempts at leaving are often helpful in terms of the victim gathering information about support services and tactics to stay safe, as well as strengthening her resolve to take this huge—and often dangerous—step. Hopefully, your expectations for what a victim should look like are more realistic now that you've considered these factors.

What You Can Do

- Always remember that leaving is a process—not an event.
- Be prepared to help women leave repeatedly, and to support them regardless of whether they stay, leave or vacillate. It's complicated. Be prepared to support a woman for as many times as it takes for her to safely leave the situation.
- Withhold judgment for the victim's choices and state. She is living in an extraordinarily frightening, confusing and overwhelming situation. It is unlikely that she will be calm, decisive and together. If you begin to feel judgmental, take a step back and consider the hell she is going through.
- Recall that the victim is the expert on the perpetrator and the level of risk. Listen to her.
- Help women take steps toward leaving, *if they feel they can*, using a safety plan (Appendix IV).
- Never make your help and support contingent upon the victim leaving.

- Never judge a woman for staying in a violent relationship. Leaving is dangerous and frightening, and there are a host of reasons why she may not be able to leave (or leave right then).
- Never minimize the risk or experience of intimate partner violence victims.
- Do everything you can to reinforce the idea that the victim has value and does not deserve to be treated the way she is treated.
- Tell the victim that you are concerned for her safety. Be there for her.
- If possible, perform a LAP (Appendix II) interview with the victim.

Discussion Ideas

1. Had you ever thought about the issues brought up in this chapter? Why or why not? Have you ever said that you would leave immediately if someone abused you?
2. What things do you tell yourself that separate you from victims of intimate partner violence?
3. Think of as many additional difficulties as you can that victims must overcome to leave. These can be everyday things, such as taking children out of their schools.
4. How can criminal justice professionals help women to leave violent relationships?
5. What are some ways that you can help a victim leave without adding pressure or your expectations for the timeline to the mix?

References and Notes

1. A. D. LaViolette and O. W. Barnett, *It Could Happen to Anyone: Why Battered Women Stay* (Newbury Park, CA: Sage, 1993).
2. B. Hart, National estimates and facts about domestic violence, *National Coalition Against Domestic Violence VOICE,* 12, 1989; S. M. Buel, Fifty obstacles to leaving, AKA, Why abuse victims stay, *The Colorado Lawyer* 28; 1999: 19–28. We are deeply indebted to S. M. Buel for this excellent article on the nuances and difficulties women face in leaving violent relationships.

3. S. M. Buel, Fifty obstacles to leaving, AKA, Why abuse victims stay, *The Colorado Lawyer* 28; 1999: 19–28.
4. X. B. Arriaga and N. M. Capezza, Targets of partner violence: The importance of understanding coping trajectories, *Journal of Interpersonal Violence* 20; 2005: 85–99, http://www.victimsclearinghouse.nsw.gov.au/Documents/89.pdf (accessed April 2, 2015).
5. Smith et al. Intimate partner homicide and corollary victims in 16 states; A. Jones, *Next Time She'll Be Dead: Battering and How to Stop It* (Boston, MA: Beacon Press, 1994); Law Enforcement News, Domestic abusers take it out on pets, too, *Law Enforcement News*, February 28; 1999: 6.
6. J. L. Dunn, *Courting Disaster: Intimate Stalking, Culture, and Criminal Justice* (New York: Aldine de Gruyter, 2002).
7. H. E. Marano, Why they stay: A saga of spouse abuse, *Psychology Today*, May/June; 1996: 56–9.
8. I. Floyd and L. Schott, *TANF Cash Benefits Continued to Lose Value in 2013* (Washington, DC: Center on Budget and Policy Priorities, 2013), http://www.cbpp.org/research/family-income-support/tanf-cash-benefits-continued-to-lose-value-in-2013 (accessed April 8, 2015). It should be noted that TANF only serves about a fourth of families below poverty level, as well. For a family of three, TANF benefits range from a high of $789 per month in New York to $271 in Texas.
9. S. Hamby, D. Finkelhor, H. Turner, and R. Ormrod, *Children's Exposure to Intimate Partner Violence and Other Family Violence* (Washington, DC: U.S. Department of Justice, 2011).
10. J. H. Grych, Children's appraisals of interparental conflict: Situational and contextual influences, *Journal of Family Psychology* 12; 1998: 437–53.
11. I. W. Hutchison and J. D. Hirschel, The effects of children's presence on woman abuse, *Violence and Victims* 16; 2001: 3–17.
12. R. I. Abrams and J. M. Greeney, *Gender Bias Study of the Supreme Judicial Court* (Boston, MA: Supreme Judicial Court, 1989), 56.
13. S. M. Buel, Fifty obstacles to leaving, AKA, Why abuse victims stay, *The Colorado Lawyer* 28; 1999: 19–28.
14. Ibid.
15. T. L. Gillum, Exploring the link between stereotypic images and intimate partner violence in the African American Community, *Violence Against Women* 8; 2002: 64–86; E. Stark, Race, gender, and woman battering, in *Violent Crime: Assessing Race and Ethnic Differences*, ed. D. F. Hawkins (Cambridge, MA: Cambridge University Press, 2003): 171–97.
16. S. M. Buel, Fifty obstacles to leaving, AKA, Why abuse victims stay, *The Colorado Lawyer* 28; 1999: 19–28.

4

Intimate Partner Violence Risk

Intimate partner violence can and does impact women from across the social and financial spectrum, though there are differences in the rates of victimization based on a number of factors. Unfortunately, people often believe that these differences mean that it is rare to see domestic violence among women in certain groups, such as the middle and upper classes, at all. While it is true that certain women are at greater risk, the truth is that intimate partner violence takes place too often even among women at lower risk for abuse. Nobody is immune from the risk of domestic violence: Intimate partner violence affects "individuals at all income levels, ethnicities, nationalities, and belief systems."[1] With that in mind, let's take a brief look at the research on victimization risk for intimate partner violence, as well as reporting issues associated with these implications.

Studies indicate that there are approximately 4.8 million women who are raped and/or physically assaulted annually, and about 1.5 million of those offenses are committed by an intimate or ex-intimate partner.[2] Women between the ages of 20 and 24 have the highest rates of intimate partner victimization, with black women reporting higher rates of victimization than women of other races.[3] In fact, black women experience intimate partner violence at a rate 35% higher than white women, though when economic and neighborhood factors are controlled for, this disparity is greatly reduced.[4] Women in households with lower incomes report domestic violence at a rate much higher than women in households with higher annual incomes regardless of race.[5] Divorced and separated people experience relationship violence at three times the rate of people who are never married.[6] Roughly 4%–8% of all pregnant women are abused by their partners during their pregnancies, and women with unwanted or unintentionally timed pregnancies are at greater risk for violent victimization.[7]

Women with physical disabilities have nearly twice the rate of all forms of domestic abuse as women without disabilities.[8]

One in five female high school students report experiencing physical and/or sexual intimate partner dating violence, and the impact on an adolescent's well-being are pernicious.[9] Teen girls who experience physical and sexual intimate partner violence are significantly more likely to have sexually transmitted infections,[10] to forego health care,[11] and to become pregnant than girls who do not experience abuse.[12] A fourth of teen girls in violent relationships report that their perpetrator is trying to get them pregnant.[13] Girls who experience intimate partner violence that is sexual are more likely to initiate sex before the age of 13, have sexual intercourse with four or more partners, and use drugs and alcohol before sex.[14]

College students also experience high rates of intimate partner violence. One study found that 42% of their sample of male and female faculty members reported receiving at least one student disclosure of a domestic violence-related incident.[15] Further, one in five college students have personally experienced intimate partner violence.[16] Given the age group most likely to experience domestic violence, it is not surprising to see such a high rate of victimization. The fact that these are college students is also suggestive of underreporting among the middle and upper classes. While this level of risk is definitely unacceptable, it is important to remember that individuals in the same age group who are not college students have a higher risk.

There is also an increased risk for intimate partner violence in couples where there is a pronounced age discrepancy—where the man is at least 16 years older than the woman, or the women is at least 10 years older than the man.[17] In the former case, it is likely that the man was drawn to the woman because it is easier to control someone much younger, who has little experience in relationships to judge their relative health, and will naturally look up to the perpetrator as someone older and wiser. The offender will likely tell the victim that he is attracted to her because she is so mature for her age, but the truth is that the attraction is quite the opposite. In the case of older women and younger men, the offender is likely to play on her insecurities regarding the age difference, promoting the idea that she is lucky to have him, or might not be able to attract another partner if he were to leave her. In this manner, both differences can be exploited to increase control over victims.

Repeat victimization and co-occurrence is common in intimate partner violence, as well.[18] One study set the rate of co-occurrence among parents at 40.7% for both intimate partner violence and child maltreatment.[19] Violence does not stay put in the confines of a home; in a sizable minority of cases, the control and abuse touches everyone in more than just psychological ways. Some of this is undoubtedly due to defensive violence and a generalized propensity for violent conflict resolution that pervades the family dynamic.

Women in small rural towns report the highest prevalence of intimate partner violence, while women in large rural towns report the lowest.[20] Geographic location is one of the many factors that influences the experience of intimate partner violence for victims. For example, isolating a victim through disabling or taking her car is very effective in a rural environment, and the added privacy afforded in a rural setting might result in a reduced chance of intervention by third parties, such as neighbors, who are less likely to hear or see altercations. Further, it is likely that people living in rural communities hold more conservative values that stress "self-reliance, 'standing by your man,' and family and group loyalty," all of which might increase the risk for intimate partner violence.[21] Traditional values and male entitlement can be a dangerous combination when it comes to domestic violence.

Employment—or, specifically, the lack thereof—has a consistent impact on intimate partner violence. This employment effect appears to be dynamic: Partners who are employed are less likely than their unemployed counterparts to both perpetrate and be victimized in the context of an intimate relationship.[22]

Intimate partner homicide committed by a male is nine times more likely in cohabitating or common law relationships than in legal marriages.[23] Other important factors that increase risk include estrangement or separation, whether the perpetrator owns a gun or threatens to kill the victim, and forced sex.[24] Two other significant risk factors are living in a lower-income neighborhood and living in an urban area—both feature higher rates of intimate partner homicide.[25]

Of male homicide victims, there is a substantial rate of victim precipitation, with roughly 30% being the first to use force in the lethal altercation.[26] Further, victims with a criminal history are more likely to provoke an intimate partner homicide than victims without prior offenses.[27] Uxoricide—the killing of one's wife—usually involves a male killing a married intimate and then killing himself, though very often that intimate is estranged.[28] In 27.2% of femicides (the killing of a woman), the perpetrator commits suicide after the homicide.[29] These victims tend to be older than the victims of acquaintance and stranger homicides, with a mean age of 35 years.[30]

Previous intimate partner violence is a common factor in nearly all intimate partner homicides.[31] Other risk factors include access to firearms, estrangement, unemployment, threats to kill, threats with a weapon, previous nonfatal strangulation, and a stepchild in the home.[32] At least intimate partner homicides are more likely to be cleared by police than cases featuring other types of perpetrators, such as strangers or friends.[33] In general, black partners have a significantly greater risk of being killed by their partners than do white partners.[34]

One study in Los Angeles found that nearly 25% of reported intimate partner violence cases over an 8-month period involved the use of a weapon. The researchers found that, of the almost 60,000 domestic violence calls to 911, 13.5% involved a dangerous weapon such as a firearm or knife.[35]

A Note on Men as Victims of Intimate Partner Violence: Show Me the Bodies

Currently, there is a sometimes rancorous dispute raging over the victimization of men in intimate relationships, and these discussions have been raging hotter since the inception of the men's movement. On one hand, you have some groups who say that men are practically never subject to violence outside of self-defense, while on the other, you have men's groups who say that the violence men face is equal or greater than that faced by women. As with most things in life, the truth tends to be found in the grayer areas, and in this discussion, we hope to shed light on the relationship between sex and intimate partner violence to the extent possible in the light of current research.

Overall, while men are the subjects of violence perpetrated by women, and not infrequently, that victimization has a dramatically different character than the abuse inflicted on women.[36] The difficulties in assessing the extent of the problem lie in definitions of abuse and violence, reporting problems, and the legal and policy implications of this area of research. The title of the chapter refers to an important distinction between the violence perpetrated by men and women that is not controversial among criminologists and criminal justice professionals: the disjuncture in the level of seriousness in such crimes at the level of lethal violence. It is indisputable that women are killed by their intimate partners at a far higher rate than men.[37]

Of the 3032 homicides involving a female victim in 2010, 39% were committed by an intimate partner, 37% were committed by a non-intimate (24% were committed by an unknown offender). In the same year, of the 10,878 homicides involving male victims, 3% were committed by an intimate partner, 48% by a non-intimate (50% were committed by an offender with an unknown relationship to the victim).[38] The difference (39% versus 3%) is enormous, and represents a serious blow to the argument that women are as, or more, violent than men in the context of intimate relationships.[39]

That said, there are numerous surveys that show that women commit as much—and even more—violence than men in intimate relationships short of that with a lethal resolution,[40] while many others find that intimate partner violence is largely perpetrated by men against their female intimates and ex-intimates.[41] Here, it appears that, by many measures, women do commit more violence against intimate partners than was previously believed. The key is in unpacking whether women engage in what is called "common couple violence" or what is called "patriarchal terrorism."[42]

The idea is that couples sometimes fight, and that fighting can sometimes escalate to physical violence such as pushing, shoving and hitting, but that violence is not characterized by the control and terroristic tactics used in abuse referred to as patriarchal terrorism. Common couple violence does not feature the fear and power dynamic that characterizes patriarchal terrorism. This is a useful distinction in understanding the violence of women as well as men. Our position in this fray is that the vast majority of violence perpetrated by women falls in the category of common couple violence or self-defense, while the violence of men is split among the categories of common couple violence, patriarchal terrorism and, to a lesser degree, self-defense.

This distinction matters a great deal, because the consequences and harm involved in common couple violence are significantly reduced relative to patriarchal terrorism, while self-defense is justified and unavoidable. Another key distinction between these types of violence is a pattern of control that only exists in the case of patriarchal terrorism. If both partners feel free to use violence against one another in a common couple altercation, it is problematic, but far less so than the situation where one partner is so cowed that violence is only used in self-defense or not at all.

One of the bedrocks to the idea that men are victimized in kind by women—known as gender symmetry—is that male intimate violence victims are too ashamed and embarrassed to come forward and report their abuse, and as such, the statistics are underreporting women's abusive behavior by significant amounts. However, this makes little sense in light of what we know about how men and women report. Research indicates that female victims of intimate partner violence tend to minimize and underreport their own abuse, while male offenders tend to minimize the abuse they *perpetrate*.[43] Studies and experience shows that male perpetrators typically excuse, justify and otherwise minimize their use of violence.[44]

Further, while women are likely to be fearful about intimate partner violence (and thus less likely to report it), numerous studies indicate that men often find women's violence humorous rather than frightening.[45] If violence provokes amusement rather than fear, it is likely to be common couple violence. This is not to say that all violence by women is less serious; there is evidence that women do perpetrate some very serious violence on occasion.[46] It is simply to draw attention to the fact that this is a very rare occurrence relative to male perpetrators to the extent that there are serious injuries.

While women do engage in violence in intimate partner relationships, we do not see the impact of this in any sort of commensurate way. Men are not crippled by a loss of self-esteem due to their abuse, they are rarely physically injured to the point of requiring medical treatment, and they are not fleeing in fear of their lives because of it. The reason we do not see such men is simply because there are very, very few of them. Women manipulate and control men in relationships, and do become violent outside of the context of mutual aggression, very low-level violence, or self-defense—but they are the exception rather than the rule in the context of harm. In addition to being more likely to be killed, women are more likely than men to suffer injuries, lose time from work, require medical intervention, and be bedridden from their injuries than men.[47]

If shame prevented people from seeking help, women would be as invisible in their abuse as men. A significant number of male abusers are arrested as a result of third parties calling the police when they hear a disturbance—it makes no sense that we are not seeing arrests of women abusers for the same reason—third party reports—at higher rates if there are a significant number of them out there. Moreover, there is less of a cultural prohibition against women hitting men than the reverse, which further suggests that it is unlikely that women are underreporting their own violence while men are not underreporting theirs. Certainly, men might feel embarrassed to report abuse suffered at the hands of a female intimate, or fear they will not be believed, but this argument is valid for women suffering violence, as well, particularly given societal judgments related to class where domestic violence is concerned.

There is a difference between violence that is abusive—and thus features elements of psychological and emotional abuse—and physical violence without the added element of power and control.[48] Some studies show that intimate partner violence affects women at a significantly higher rate than men: Roughly 85% of victims are women, and women are at significantly higher risk of sustaining serious injuries than men.[49] No matter which partner is killed, in 70%–80% of intimate partner homicides, the man physically abused the woman prior to the murder.[50] On the other hand, the National Intimate Partner and Sexual Violence Survey (NISVS) shows that more men (53%) than women are victims of intimate partner violence.[51] The National Violence Against Women Survey (NVAWS), on the other hand, puts the number of male victims at 38%.[52] It has been suggested that the different findings resulted because the former is presented to respondents as a crime survey, while the latter is presented as a health survey.[53]

Women are more likely to use a weapon than are men, and this finding appears to be fairly consistent across surveys; from 2002 to 2011, a greater percentage of men (27%) than women (18%) were victimized by their intimate partners using a weapon. Similarly, 5% of women and 19% of men were hit by an object their intimate partner held or threw at them.[54] This makes sense as women are generally at a physical disadvantage to their male partners, and thus would be more likely to use a weapon of some sort to even the playing field. Unfortunately, the use of a weapon interjects more danger of injury in an already violent situation, and this finding is used by the men's movement to perpetrate the idea that women are more abusive than men.

It is believed that the prevalence for abuse in same-sex relationships is high, though there are few studies focusing on the problem to date.[55] However, there are important differences in same-sex violence with respect to gender: While intimate partner violence among gay and bisexual men occurs at similar and perhaps even higher rates than in heterosexual relationships, with 32% reporting either physical violence or unwanted sexual activity, lesbians report similar abuse in only 11% of their relationships compared to 30.4% for heterosexual women.[56,57] The implications do not speak well of male socialization, nor the notion that women push men to perpetrate violence against them.

Therapists who work with male intimate violence perpetrators will tell you that they enjoy playing the role of the victim.[58] They have numerous excuses for their abusive behavior that cast them in that role, as we saw in Chapter 2. It is not uncommon for them to characterize themselves as the abused party, and to call attention to wounds where they exist, even when they were inflicted by a female partner in self-defense. This often leads to dual arrests where mandatory arrest policies are in place, and there has been a significant increase in the number of women being arrested alongside her abuser if she fights back or leaves any visible marks for police to see.[59] Law enforcement officers acknowledge the difference in male versus female violence in Susan Miller's[59] research:

> Most did not see women as primary aggressors, and no one felt that women were able to achieve the power and control over their male partners that are typically in place in relationships where the male batters the female .... What is most telling is how many respondents from both groups [police and criminal justice professionals] mentioned that they do not encounter male "victims" who are "bloody, bruised, and broken" the way they find female victims.[60]

The context in which the violence takes place is crucial in making sense of these disparate findings. One person's report of hitting an intimate partner might be categorically different than the same report from another person. At the same time, it is important to begin acknowledging the existence of male intimates who are subject to serious abuse by their partners, and providing resources for them to avoid victimization, along with women. While we believe that, taken in context, women's serious violence against their male intimate partners is far less common than a couple of these survey instruments would suggest, there are certainly women who break the existing pattern. When men call for help, it is ridiculous to treat them in a manner that we would find unacceptable were the victim a woman.

What You Can Do

- Educate others about the universal nature of the risk for intimate partner violence.
- Help obviate the risk of forced pregnancy in victims of intimate partner violence by assisting them in obtaining discreet, long-term birth control options.
- Help fight misinformation on the topic of gender differences in intimate partner violence and homicide.
- Inform people that, while women do engage in relationship violence, the seriousness of this violence is only rarely on par with that of male perpetrators.
- The injury and harm caused by male perpetrators is such that an appropriate response to the suggestion that women commit as much relationship violence as men might be "Show me the bodies."
- Check on the availability of services and support for male victims of intimate partner violence in your area. Though rare, men can face abuse, and need to be believed when they report it.

Discussion Ideas

1. Why do you think that intimate partner violence is so widely believed to be a strictly lower-class phenomenon? How does this belief change our reactions to it as a society?
2. Research the men's movement and the feminist movement—what are the key differences between the two? Where are they similar? Why would members of the men's movement *want* to

see higher rates of female-perpetrated violence? Why would members of the feminist movement push back against this assertion?

3. Black victims are faced with an extra burden when reporting intimate partner violence coupled with higher rates of such violence. What can we do to make it easier for them to reach out for help?
4. As you saw in this chapter, intimate partner violence can start very early. What sorts of messages should we be conveying to high school and middle school students about this type of crime?
5. What are some of the special challenges in being a victim with few financial resources? What are some of the challenges in being a victim with ample financial resources? What special considerations do children bring to a violent situation? Pets? Try to really put yourself in the shoes of victims with these factors at play.

References and Notes

1. T. N. Sulak, T. F. Saxon, and D. Fearon, Applying the theory of reasoned action to domestic violence reporting behavior: The role of sex and victimization, *Journal of Family Violence* 29(2); 2014: 165–73.
2. M. Lundy and S. F. Grossman, Domestic violence service users: A comparison of older and younger women victims, *Journal of Family Violence* 24; 2009: 297–309; J. Sullivan and N. Websdale, Domestic violence fatality review teams: An interprofessional model to reduce deaths. *Journal of Interprofessional Care* 20(5); 2006: 535–44.
3. C. A. Franklin and G. A. Kercher, The intergenerational transmission of intimate partner violence: Differentiating correlates in a random community sample, *Journal of Family Violence* 27; 2012: 187–99; C. M. Rennison and S. Welchans, *Intimate Partner Violence* (Washington, DC: U.S. Department of Justice, 2000), http://www.atria.nl/epublications/2000/intimate_partner_violence.pdf (accessed March 23, 2015).
4. P. Tjaden and N. Thoennes, *Extent, Nature, and Consequences of Intimate Partner Violence: Findings From the National Violence Against Women Survey* (Washington, DC: U.S. Department of Justice, 2000); M. L. Benson and G. L. Fox, *When Violence Hits Home: How Economics and Neighborhood Play a Role* (Washington, DC: U.S. Department of Justice, 2004).
5. Ibid.
6. Ibid.

7. J. A. Gazmararian, R. Petersen, A. M. Spitz, M. M. Goodwin, L. E. Saltzman, and J. S. Marks, Violence and reproductive health: Current knowledge and future research directions, *Maternal and Child Health Journal* 4; 2000: 79–84; R. E. Gee, N. Mitra, F. Wan, D. E. Chavkin, and J. A. Long, Power over parity: Intimate partner violence and issues of fertility control, *American Journal of Obstetrics and Gynecology* 201; 2009: 148.e1–7; J. L. Jasinski, Pregnancy and domestic violence: A review of the literature, *Trauma, Violence, and Abuse* 5; 2004: 47–64.
8. D. L. Smith, Disability, gender and intimate partner violence: Relationships from the behavioral risk factor surveillance system, *Sexuality and Disability* 26; 2008: 15–28.
9. J. G. Silverman, A. Raj, L. A. Mucci, and J. E. Hathaway, Dating violence against adolescent girls and associated substance use, unhealthy weight control, sexual risk behavior, pregnancy, and suicidality, *JAMA* 286; 2001: 572–9.
10. M. R. Decker, J. G. Silverman, and A. Raj, Dating violence and sexually transmitted disease/HIV testing and diagnosis among adolescent females, *Pediatrics* 116; 2005: e272–6.
11. E. Miller, M. R. Decker, A. Raj, E. Reed, D. Marable, and J. G. Silverman, Intimate partner violence and health care-seeking patterns among female users of urban adolescent clinics, *Maternal and Child Health Journal* 14; 2010: 910–17.
12. T. A. Roberts, P. Auinger, and J. D. Klein, Intimate partner abuse and the reproductive health of sexually active female adolescents, *Journal of Adolescent Health* 36; 2005: 380–5; A. L. Coker, Does physical intimate partner violence affect sexual health? A systematic review, *Trauma, Violence and Abuse* 8; 2007: 149–77.
13. E. Miller, M. R. Decker, H. L. McCauley, D. J. Tancredi, R. R. Levenson, J. Waldman, P. Schoenwal, and J. G. Silverman, Pregnancy coercion, intimate partner violence, and unintended pregnancy, *Contraception* 81; 2010: 316–22; E. Miller, B. Jordan, R. Levenson, and J. G. Silverman, Reproductive coercion: Connecting the dots between partner violence and unintended pregnancy, *Contraception* 81; 2010: 457–9.
14. Y. S. Kim-Godwin, C. Clements, A. M. McCuiston, and J. A. Fox, Dating violence among high school students in Southeastern North Carolina, *Journal of School Nursing* 25; 2009: 141–51.
15. T. N. Richards, K. A. Branch, and R. M. Hayes, An exploratory examination of student to professor disclosures of crime victimization, *Violence Against Women* 19; 2013: 1408–22.
16. Ibid.
17. N. Breitman, T. K. Shackelford, and C. R. Block, Couple age discrepancy and risk of intimate partner homicide, *Violence and Victims* 19; 2004: 321–33.
18. There are even instances of multiple perpetrator intimate violence, which account for one in 10 physical assaults and one in five aggravated assaults on women. M. Salter, Multi-perpetrator domestic violence, *Trauma, Violence and Abuse* 15; 2014: 102–12.

19. W. E. Goodlin and C. S. Dunn, Three patterns of domestic violence in households: Single victimization, repeat victimization, and co-occurring victimization, *Journal of Family Violence* 25; 2010: 107–22.
20. K. Harland, C. Peek-Asa, A. Wallis, K. Beyer, P. Dickey, and A. Saftlas, Rural disparity in domestic violence prevalence and access to resources, *Journal of Women's Health* 20; 2011: 1743–9. Though it should be noted that intimate partner violence is more likely to result in homicide in urban areas.
21. S. F. Grossman, S. Hinkley, A. Kawalski, and C. Margrave, Rural versus urban victims of violence: The interplay of race and region, *Journal of Family Violence* 20; 2005: 71–81.
22. C. A. Franklin and G. A. Kercher, The intergenerational transmission of intimate partner violence: Differentiating correlates in a random community sample, *Journal of Family Violence* 27; 2012: 187–99.
23. K. Mize, T. Shackelford, and V. Weekes-Shackelford, Hands-on killing of intimate partners as a function of sex and relationship status/state, *Journal of Family Violence* 24; 2009: 463–70.
24. J. C. Campbell, N. Glass, P. W. Sharps, K. Laughon, and T. Bloom, Intimate partner homicide, *Trauma, Violence and Abuse* 8; 2007: 246–69.
25. C. Diem and J. M. Pizarro, Social structure and family homicides, *Journal of Family Violence* 25; 2010: 521–32.
26. L. R. Muftic and D. E. Hunt, Victim precipitation: Further understanding the linkage between victimization and offending in homicide, *Homicide Studies* 17; 2013: 239–54.
27. Ibid.
28. F. Stephen Bridges and W. B. Tankersley, Mean ages of homicide victims and victims of homicide-suicide, *Psychological Reports* 106; 2010: 163–9.
29. T. N. Richards, L. K. Gillespie, and E. M. Givens, Reporting femicide-suicide in the news: The current utilization of suicide reporting guidelines and recommendations for the future, *Journal of Family Violence* 29; 2014: 453–63.
30. R. Panczak, M. Geissbuhler, M. Zwahlen, M. Killias, K. Tal, and M. Egger, Homicide-suicides compared to homicides and suicides: Systemic and meta-analysis, *Forensic Science International* 233; 2013: 28–36.
31. Ibid.
32. S. G. Smith, K. A. Fowler, and P. H. Niolon, Intimate partner homicide and corollary victims in 16 states: National violent death reporting system, *American Journal of Public Health* 104; 2014: 461–8, http://www.researchgate.net/profile/Sharon_Smith19/publication/259768650_Intimate_Partner_Homicide_and_Corollary_Victims_in_16_States_National_Violent_Death_Reporting_System_2003-2009/links/5422b3540cf238c6ea6ae188.pdf (accessed November 6, 2014).
33. K. Quinet and S. Nunn, Establishing the victim-offender relationship of initially unsolved homicides: Partner, family, acquaintance, or stranger, *Homicide Studies* 18; 2014: 271–97.

34. P. Kernsmith and S. W. Craun, Predictors of weapon use in domestic violence incidents reported to law enforcement, *Journal of Family Violence* 23; 2008: 589–96.
35. Ibid.
36. S. L. Miller, *Criminalized Conduct: The Paradox of Women Arrested for Domestic Violence* (New Brunswick, NJ: Rutgers University Press, 2005).
37. C. M. Rennison, *Intimate Partner Violence, 1992–2001, Bureau of Justice Statistics Crime Brief* (Washington, DC: U.S. Department of Justice, 2002).
38. S. Catalano, *Intimate Partner Violence: Attributes of Victimization, 1993–2011* (Washington, DC: U.S. Department of Justice, 2013).
39. This relationship does not vary significantly from year-to-year, though there has been a significant decline in female-perpetrated intimate partner homicides relative to male-perpetrated intimate partner homicides in the years since domestic violence services became widespread.
40. For example, see L. D. Brush, Violent acts and injurious outcomes in married couples: Methodological issues in the national survey of families and households, *Gender and Society* 4; 1990: 56–67; R. Caetano, S. Ramisetty-Mikler, and C. A. Field, Unidirectional and bidirectional intimate partner violence among, black, white, and Hispanic couples in the U.S., *Violence and Victims* 20; 2005: 398–406; R. Caetano, J. Schafer, C. A. Field, and S. M. Nelson, Agreements on reports of intimate partner violence among black, white, and Hispanic couples in the United States, *Journal of Interpersonal Violence* 17; 2002: 1308–22; J. J. Cercone, S. R. H. Beach, and I. Arias, Gender symmetry in dating intimate partner violence: Does similar behavior imply similar constructs? *Violence and Victims* 20; 2005: 207–18; K. A. Chase, T. J. O'Farrell, C. M. Murphy, W. Fals-Stewart, and M. Murphy, Factors associated with partner violence among female alcoholic patients and their male partners, *Journal of Studies on Alcohol* 64; 2003: 137–49; C. B. Cunradi, M. Bersamin, and G. Ames, Agreement on interpersonal violence among a sample of blue collar couples, *Journal of Interpersonal Violence* 24; 2008: 551–68; B. H. Hoff, U.S. national survey: More men than women victims of intimate partner violence, *Journal of Aggression, Conflict and Peace Research* 4; 2012: 155–63; L. Madgol, T. E. Moffitt, A. Caspi, J. Fajan, and P. A. Silva, Gender differences in partner violence in a birth cohort of 21-year-olds: Bridging the gap between clinical and epidemiological approaches, *Journal of Counseling and Clinical Psychology* 65; 1997: 68–78.
41. See, for example, L. K. Hamberger and C. E. Guse, Women's and men's use of intimate partner violence in clinical samples, *Violence Against Women* 8; 2002: 1301–31; L. K. Hamberger, and T. Potente, Counseling heterosexual women arrested for domestic violence: Implications for theory and practice, *Violence and Victims* 9; 1994: 125–37; K. Henning and L. Feder, A comparison between men and women arrested for domestic violence: Who presents the greater threat? *Journal of Family Violence* 19; 2004: 69–81; S. L. Miller, The paradox of women arrested for domestic violence: Criminal justice professionals and service providers respond,

Violence Against Women 7; 2001: 1339–76; P. Tjaden and N. Theonnes, Prevalence and consequences of male-to-female and female-to-male intimate partner violence as measured by the national violence against women survey, *Violence Against Women* 6; 2000: 142–61.

42. M. P. Johnson, Patriarchal terrorism and common couple violence: Two forms of violence against women, *Journal of Marriage and the Family* 57; 1995: 283–94. Johnson was making the assertion that a significant amount of domestic violence occurred in the context of common couple violence. The distinction has also been referred to as the family violence and feminist perspectives. M. A. Straus, Some social antecedents of physical punishment: A linkage theory interpretation, *Journal of Marriage and the Family* 33; 1971: 658–63; R. E. Dobash and R. P. Dobash, *Violence Against Wives* (New York: Free Press, 1979).
43. See J. Belknap and H. Melton, *Are Heterosexual Men Also Victims of Intimate Partner Violence?* (Washington, DC: Violence against Women National Online Resource Center, 2005), http://www.vawnet.org/Assoc_Files_VAWnet/AR_MaleVictims.pdf (accessed May 28, 2014); N. Berns, Degendering the problem and gendering the blame: Political discourse on women and violence, *Gender and Society* 15; 2000: 262–81; J. C. Campbell, *Assessing Dangerousness: Violence by Sexual Offenders, Batterers, and Child Abusers* (Thousand Oaks, CA: Sage, 1995); R. P. Dobash, R. E. Dobash, K. Cavanagh, and R. Lewis, Separate and intersecting realities: A comparison of men's and women's accounts of violence against women, *Violence Against Women* 4; 1998: 382–414; S. Goodrum, D. Umberson, and K. L. Anderson, The batterer's view of self and others in domestic violence, *Sociological Inquiry* 71; 2001: 221–40; D. A. Heckert and E. W. Gondolf, Predictors of underreporting of male violence by batterer program participants and their partners, *Journal of Family Violence* 15; 2000: 423–43.
44. R. P. Dobash, R. E. Dobash, M. Wilson, and M. Daly, The myth of sexual symmetry in marital violence, *Social Problems* 39; 1992: 71–91; K. Henning, A. Jones, and R. Holford, 'I didn't do it, but if I did I had a good reason': Minimization, denial, and attributes of blame among male and female domestic violence offenders, *Journal of Family Violence* 20; 2005: 131–9.
45. L. K. Hamberger and C. E. Guse, Women's and men's use of intimate partner violence in clinical samples, *Violence Against Women* 8; (2002): 1301–31; M. O'Keefe and L. Treister, Victims of dating violence among high school students: Are the predictors different for males and females, *Violence Against Women* 4; 1998: 195–223.
46. M. A. Straus, Women's violence toward men is a serious social problem, in *Current Controversies in Family Violence,* eds. D. R. Loseke, R. J. Gelles, and M. M. Cavanaugh (Thousand Oaks, CA: Sage, 2005), 55–77.
47. J. Archer, Sex differences in aggression between heterosexual partners: A meta-analytic review, *Psychological Bulletin* 126; 2000: 651–80; R. A. Berk, S. F. Berk, D. R. Loseke, and D. Rauma, Combat and other family violence myths, in *The Dark Side of Families: Current Violence*

Research, eds. D. Finkelhor, R. J. Gelles, G. T. Hoteling, and M. A. Straus (Beverly Hills, CA: Sage, 1983), 197–212; A. E. Bonomi, M. L. Anderson, F. P. Rivara, and R. S. Thompson, Health outcomes in women with physical and sexual intimate partner violence exposure, *Journal of Women's Health* 16; 2007: 987–97; Brush, Violent acts and injurious outcomes in married couples; J. C. Campbell, Health consequences of intimate partner violence, *Lancet* 359; 2002: 1331–6; C. A. Cook and R. J. Harris, Attributions about spouse abuse cases of bidirectional battering, *Violence and Victims* 10; 1995: 143–51; H. Johnson and V. P. Bunge, Prevalence and consequences of spousal assault in Canada, *Canadian Journal of Criminology* 43; 2001: 27–45.

48. See J. Belknap and H. Melton, *Are Heterosexual Men Also Victims of Intimate Partner Violence?* (Washington, DC: Violence against Women National Online Resource Center, 2005); M. P. Johnson, Patriarchal terrorism and common couple violence: Two forms of violence against women, *Journal of Marriage and the Family* 57; 1995: 283–94.
49. M. C. Black, K. C. Basile, M. J. Breiding, S. G. Smith, M. L. Walters, M. T. Merrick, J. Chen, and M. R. Stevens, *The National Intimate Partner and Sexual Violence Survey: 2010 Summary Report* (National Center for Injury Prevention and Control. Atlanta, GA: Centers for Disease Control and Prevention, 2011), http://www.cdc.gov/violenceprevention/pdf/nisvs_report2010-a.pdf (accessed February 12, 2015). M. R. Durose, C. W. Harlow, P. A. Langan, M. Motivans, R. R. Rantala, and E. L. Smith, *Family Violence Statistics Including Statistics on Strangers and Acquaintances* (Washington, DC: U.S. Department of Justice, 2005).
50. J. C. Campbell, D. Webster, J. Koziol-McLain, C. R. Block, D. Campbell, M. A. Curry … and S. A. Wilt, *Assessing Risk Factors for Intimate Partner Homicide* (Washington, DC: US Department of Justice, 2003), https://www.ncjrs.gov/pdffiles1/jr000250e.pdf (accessed January 13, 2015).
51. M. C. Black, K. C. Basile, M. J. Breiding, S. G. Smith, M. L. Walters, M. T. Merrick, J. Chen, and M. R. Stevens, *The National Intimate Partner and Sexual Violence Survey: 2010 Summary Report* (National Center for Injury Prevention and Control. Atlanta, GA: Centers for Disease Control and Prevention, 2011), http://www.cdc.gov/violenceprevention/pdf/nisvs_report2010-a.pdf (accessed February 12, 2015).
52. B. H. Hoff, U.S. national survey: More men than women victims of intimate partner violence, *Journal of Aggression, Conflict and Peace Research* 4; 2012: 155–63.
53. However, it seems unlikely that the distinction in the surveys would affect men and women's reporting at differential rates. Both might be less likely to report violence as a crime rather than as a health issue. M. A. Straus, Women's violence toward men is a serious social problem, in *Current Controversies in Family Violence*, eds. D. R. Loseke, R. J. Gelles, and M. M. Cavanaugh (Thousand Oaks, CA: Sage, 2005), 55–77.

54. S. Catalano, *Intimate Partner Violence: Attributes of Victimization, 1993–2011* (Washington, DC: U.S. Department of Justice, 2013).
55. C. Brown, Gender-role implications on same-sex intimate partner abuse, *Journal of Family Violence* 23; 2008: 457–62.
56. E. Houston and D. J. McKirnan, Intimate partner abuse among gay and bisexual men: Risk correlates and health outcomes, *Journal of Urban Health* 84; 2007: 681–90.
57. National Center for Injury Prevention and Control, *Costs of Intimate Partner Violence Against Women in the United States* (Atlanta, GA: Centers for Disease Control and Prevention, 2003).
58. L. Bancroft, *Why Does He Do That? Inside the Minds of Angry and Controlling Men* (New York: Berkley Books, 2003).
59. R. F. Marcus, Patterns of intimate partner violence in young adult couples: Nonviolent, unilaterally violent, and mutually violent couples, *Violence and Victims* 27; 2012: 299–314; S. L. Miller, *Victims as Offenders: The Paradox of Women's Violence in Relationships* (New Brunswick, NJ: Rutgers University Press, 2005).
60. Ibid, 89.

5

Gimme Shelter

Responding to Intimate Partner Violence

When it comes to domestic violence, everybody is a potential first responder. Unfortunately, most of us are woefully unprepared for that important role. The initial responses to a woman breaking her silence about domestic violence are terribly important in securing her safety. After reading this chapter you will be in a position to represent a positive influence in her move from victim to survivor. Even when women are not ready to share about their victimization, you can have a positive impact on their sense of self that may come to fruition down the road. One of the most important things we have to do as individuals, and as a society, is recognize and acknowledge intimate partner victimization, no matter how uncomfortable it might make us. In addition to suggestions for individuals responding to domestic violence, this section presents responses for policy makers, and those in a position to influence policy.

Functional Limitations

One of the most important things for those responding to intimate violence to understand is the functional limitations incurred by victims through exposure to intimate partner violence. Aside from physical injury, it has been linked to a variety of negative mental health outcomes, such as depression, anxiety, antisocial behavioral patterns, aggression, low self-esteem and substance abuse.[1] These functional limitations may be hidden, so those responding to intimate partner violence might not be aware that the victim is not functioning at an optimal, or even their normal, level.[2] Be gentle. Imagine it was you in the situation—exhausted, scared, depressed—trying to cope with a frightening situation, quite possibly with little hope that anyone will be able to help. The two services most commonly requested by victims are emotional support and legal assistance.[3] If you are not a domestic violence professional, the key is to encourage victims to report their abuse to those professionals who are prepared and willing to assist them through their crisis. Community education is crucial in this respect, particularly in less urban areas where victims more often rely on family and friends as referral sources.[4]

The folks at the Family Justice Center point out another important thing to remember: It is a myth that intimate partner violence victims do not want to talk about what is happening to them.[5] While it is true that some victims try to hide their abuse, they often do so because they fear embarrassment, the perpetrator finding out, being blamed for the violence, not being believed, or being pressured to do something they aren't prepared to do yet (such as leave the offender). What victims fear is a *poor* response to opening up—not opening up itself. Most victims desperately need emotional support and a nonjudgmental ear; they want to be asked if they are okay, because they are not, and it feels terrible to be in obvious distress while those around you seem to ignore your plight. Listen, express concern, offer to help in whatever ways you can, but do not blame, pressure the victim to do what you think is right, or place conditions on your support.

Do the Legwork

One way that you can be of invaluable assistance to a victim of intimate partner violence is to help her gather information about available resources, such as shelters and advocates, and/or financial or other assistance for which she might qualify, such as childcare, Women, Infants, and Children (WIC), Temporary Assistance for Needy Families (TANF) and the like. When you are overwhelmed and depressed, it is difficult to conjure the energy and motivation to investigate such options, but it also might be difficult due to constraints imposed by the perpetrator (a lack of privacy or the time to do the necessary research, and/or fear that the offender will catch her doing that research). If you can help hook the victim up with assistance and hope, the domestic violence professionals can help her from there with information. Even if the only thing you have time to do is to provide her with her local hotline number, you have connected her with a host of resources through that entity.

Help Her Make a Safety Plan

If the victim is ready to reach out to an advocate, they can help her make a safety plan. If she isn't ready to reach out, you can help her with a safety plan at home using the resources provided in Appendix IV. Again, help her do the legwork, locating some of the phone numbers she will need, and helping her think through the worksheet located in the appendices to come up with a good plan to stay as safe as possible until she is ready to leave. If the victim is ready to leave, a safety plan is an excellent first step in planning her exit from the abusive relationship.

Orders of Protection

Orders of protection—which might be called last wills and testaments since they so often result in exactly the violence that women predict in the application—are of some use in protecting women from violent and controlling intimate partners, showing some positive protective effects, especially in the case of less violent offenders. A study in Texas covering a 2-year period before and after issuance of a protective order showed a drop in physical abuse from 68% to 23% after the order was obtained, and as long as victims maintained the order.[6] The positive effect was greater in cases where the perpetrator was arrested at the time the order was issued, but diminished if the couple had children.[7] This is likely because the presence of children makes it more difficult to keep firm boundaries in place due to custody issues (both legal and extralegal). However, it is important to note that such studies cannot determine whether the violence would have declined naturally over time in the absence of an order of protection as a result of the woman leaving.

Several studies in Seattle compared women who were abused, but did not obtain an Order of Protection, to women who did obtain orders. The first found that women were less likely to be physically abused with permanent orders than women with no orders. Women with temporary orders did not fare as well, however: They were more likely to be psychologically abused than women with no order at all. It is likely that the offender saw the temporary orders, which lasted only two weeks, as a deadline for bringing the woman to heel so that she would let the order expire. This study did not account for violations of orders that did not involve physical assaults.[8]

Other studies have found that there was no difference in women maintaining orders of protection, letting them lapse, or seeking permanent orders.[9] The second Seattle study found that orders of protection significantly reduced contact, threats with weapons, injuries and the need for medical care, but were more effective starting 9 months after the order was issued.[10] A Rhode Island study produced similar findings.[11] Specific caveats in orders of protection appear to make a difference: One study found that orders that prohibited abusive contact but not all contact led to a higher likelihood of subsequent abuse for victims in the forms of psychological and physical violence, sexual coercion and injuries within 1 year.[12]

Overall, an important and consistent finding across studies is that victims express a great deal of satisfaction with orders of protection, even when they have to call the police to report violations.[13] In one study, a victim expressed the sense that the Order of Protection sent the message to the abuser that the "law was on her side."[14] Victims reported that the Order of Protection seemed to improve their overall well-being—particularly in cases where the perpetrator was more likely to inflict subsequent harm, and had a prior criminal record.[15] While orders do not have a significant and consistent impact on subsequent abuse, they do make it easier for police to respond to calls for help (and have a reason to arrest), and seem to provide a feeling of validation and empowerment for victims.[16] While they are far from perfect, orders of protection appear to be well worth the effort to obtain in most cases.

Guns

Guns are also an important factor in saving the lives of victims of intimate partner violence. One study in 16 states and the District of Columbia found that 38% fewer women were shot to death by their partners because background checks are now required for every handgun sale.[17] Push to amend state laws so that people convicted of intimate partner violence-related crimes are included in the list of those prohibited from owning or possessing a firearm. A significant number of women are killed by intimate partners with a firearm—the presence of a gun greatly increases the probability of death in a situation in which there is intimate partner violence.[18] In fact, domestic assault involving a firearm is 12 times more likely to result in death compared to an assault involving other weapons or bodily force,[19] and an abused victim is five times more likely to be killed if their intimate partner owns a firearm.[20]

The research is fairly clear on this point: Getting guns out of the hands of perpetrators reduces intimate partner homicide dramatically. Anything you can do to encourage legislation that calls for background checks specific to such charges will have a positive impact. This is an extraordinarily important facet in saving lives.

Domestic Offender Registry

One controversial approach to reducing intimate partner violence that has drawn the attention of policy makers is instituting domestic violence registries in much the same manner that we currently register sex offenders. In order to qualify for inclusion, the offender must have three convictions for domestic violence—a very high bar in an offense that is not taken seriously enough. As domestic violence offenders tend to repeat their patterns from one relationship to the next, registries are very promising as a means to help women avoid becoming romantically involved with a perpetrator, especially as offenders are unlikely to divulge this information about their past abusive behavior. At the very least, it would likely help a victim reject excuses from an offender if abuse starts, as it would be easier to view behavior as a pattern rather than an isolated violent event resulting from stress or some other factor. Significantly, it would help a woman understand that she is not the cause of her abuse.

While such registries would undoubtedly be helpful in protecting potential and actual victims, there are a number of consequences and difficulties associated with such registries that have been noted in the case of sex offender registries. First and foremost, inclusion on such a listing is incredibly stigmatizing, and while that might not be a concern we have for most perpetrators of intimate partner violence, there are cases where treatment and rehabilitation efforts are successful, and the offender is still labelled indefinitely. One way to address this potential issue would be to cull names from the list if the offender goes a specified length of time (such as ten years) without a repeat offense. As far as the stigma creating difficulties in finding a romantic partner, it is unlikely that a former perpetrator who has genuinely changed would not be forthcoming about his past history of intimate partner violence, and the road to overcoming those attitudes and behaviors, with a new partner.

Some might be concerned that an ex-partner might use the registry to get back at a spurned lover, but this is not a valid concern given the need for three convictions. With that high standard to reach for inclusion, it is more likely that the bigger problem would be that the majority of perpetrators would not warrant inclusion on the registry when they should be included.

Intimate Partner Violence Education in Schools

One of the most fundamental changes we can make with respect to the prevention of intimate partner violence is to start educating young people about the subject in our schools. Teaching students about the problem—warning signs, prevention, how to get help, how to become allies and the like—is one of the most basic steps in eradicating the problem, and yet very few schools address this serious issue. We need to encourage change in this direction, or our children and grandchildren will be facing the same problems we currently have down the road.

In addition to practical, individual-level advice, this education must address misogyny and the prevailing attitude that domestic violence is somehow less important than other varieties of violence in order to truly make a difference. It is mind-boggling that there is so much resistance to the idea that women are treated differently than men in a negative sense, but that resistance has to be overcome to effect real change. Unfortunately, antifeminist rhetoric will likely make such programs difficult to institute in some venues, but it is a necessary fight. Until the issue is widely acknowledged and addressed, it is unlikely that we will see real change in the number of women hurt and killed as the result of intimate partner violence.

What You Can Do

- Support your local domestic violence shelter—they are doing hard, difficult work and are in constant need of funds, supplies and trained volunteers.

- Contact your local shelter to ask them what they need. Women often leave without much in terms of clothing, toiletries, linens, toys for children and the like, but space might be at a premium in a given shelter. Make sure that you are donating items they both need and have the space to store. Get your charitable organization, church or sports team involved to increase your impact.
- Acknowledge domestic violence when you suspect it. Victims often feel invisible and isolated, and ignoring signs of abuse only adds to this impression.
- Be gentle and patient. Imagine it was you in the situation—exhausted, scared, depressed—trying to cope with a frightening situation, quite possibly with little hope that you will be able to get help.
- Contact your local schools and suggest that age-appropriate educational programs about intimate partner violence should be a part of the curriculum in classes such as health and fitness.

Discussion Ideas

1. What can we do to get guns out of the hands of intimate partner violence perpetrators?
2. Can you think of some alternative services that might help victims of intimate partner violence beyond advocacy and shelters? Think outside the box.
3. How has social media helped or hurt the cause of intimate partner violence victims? Can you recall anything you've seen on social media about the issue? If you were tasked with creating a social media product to inform people about domestic violence, what would you want to convey?
4. Why do you think we are embarrassed in the face of intimate partner violence? Why is it so embarrassing for victims?
5. It is common to hear people characterize aggression on the part of young boys toward girls as meaning that the boys "like" the girls. Moreover, this is likely true in many cases. Think about and discuss the implications of this for intimate partner violence.

References and Notes

1. T. N. Sulak, T. F. Saxon, and D. Fearon, Applying the theory of reasoned action to domestic violence reporting behavior, *Journal of Women's Health* 20; 2014: 1743–9.
2. H. Y. Lee, E. Park, and E. Lightfoot, When does a battered woman seek help from the police? The role of battered women's functionality, *Journal of Family Violence* 25(2); 2010: 195–204.
3. S. F. Grossman, S. Hinkley, A. Kawalski, and C. Margrave, Rural versus urban victims of violence: The interplay of race and region, *Journal of Family Violence* 20; 2005: 71–81.
4. Ibid.
5. Family Justice Center, *About Domestic Violence* (Washington, DC: Family Justice Center, 2012), http://www.fjcsafe.org/about-domestic-violence (accessed June 2, 2015).
6. M. J. Carlson, S. D. Harris, and G. W. Holden, Protective orders and domestic violence: Risk factors for re-abuse, *Journal of Family Violence* 14; 1999: 205–26.
7. Ibid.
8. V. L. Holt, M. A. Kernic, T. Lumley, M. E. Wolf, and F. P. Rivara, Civil protection orders and risk of subsequent police-reported violence, *Journal of the American Medical Association* 288; 2002: 589–94.
9. A. Harrell and B. E. Smith, Effects of restraining orders on domestic violence victims, in *Do Arrest and Restraining Orders Work?* eds. E. S. Buzawa and C. G. Buzawa (Thousand Oaks, CA: Sage, 1996), 214–43; A. R. Klein, Re-abuse in a population of court-restrained male batterers: Why restraining orders don't work, in *Do Arrest and Restraining Orders Work?* eds. E. S. Buzawa and C. G. Buzawa (Thousand Oaks, CA: Sage, 1996), 192–214.
10. V. L. Holt, M. A. Kernic, M. E. Wolf, and F. P. Rivara, Do protection orders affect the likelihood of future partner violence and injury? *American Journal of Preventive Medicine* 24; 2003: 16–21.
11. A. R. Klein, D. Wilson, A. H. Crowe, and M. DeMichele, *Evaluation of the Rhode Island Probation Specialized Domestic Violence Supervision Unit* (Washington, DC: U.S. Department of Justice, 2005), https://www.ncjrs.gov/pdffiles1/nij/grants/222912.pdf (accessed July 6, 2015).
12. T. K. Logan, L. Shannon, R. Walker, and T. M. Faragher, Protective orders: Questions and conundrums, *Trauma, Violence and Abuse* 7; 2006: 175–205.
13. A. R. Klein, Re-abuse in a population of court-restrained male batterers: Why restraining orders don't work, in *Do Arrest and Restraining Orders Work?* eds. E. S. Buzawa and C. G. Buzawa (Thousand Oaks, CA: Sage, 1996), 192–214.
14. J. Ptacek, *Battered Women in the Courtroom: The Power of Judicial Responses* (Boston, MA: Northeastern University Press, 1999).

15. S. L. Keilitz, P. L. Hannaford, and H. S. Efkeman, *Civil Protection Orders: The Benefits and Limitations for Victims of Domestic Violence* (Washington, DC: U.S. Department of Justice, 1997), https://www.ncjrs.gov/pdffiles1/pr/172223.pdf (accessed July 5, 2015).
16. A. R. Klein, *Practical Implications of Current Domestic Violence Research: For Law Enforcement, Prosecutors and Judges* (Washington, DC: U.S. Department of Justice, 2009).
17. Y. Crasso, My sister's keeper: Working to reduce domestic violence and gun violence, *Women's Health Activist* 39; 2014: 1–5. S. B. Sorenson and D. J. Wiebe, Weapons in the lives of battered women, *American Journal of Public Health* 93; 2004: 1412–13; E. R. Vigdor and J. A. Mercy, Do laws restricting access to firearms by domestic violence offenders prevent intimate partner homicide? *Evaluation Review* 30; 2006: 313–32.
18. S. B. Sorenson, Firearm use in intimate partner violence: A brief overview, *Journal of Applied Social Research* 229; 2006: 232–3.
19. Bureau of Justice Statistics, *Homicide Trends in the US: Intimate Homicide* (Washington, DC: U.S. Department of Justice, 2007), http://www.lb7.uscourts.gov/documents/08-37701.pdf (accessed July 8, 2015).
20. J. C. Campbell, D. Webster, J. Koziol-McLain et al., Risk factors for femicide in abusive relationships: Results from a multisite case control study, *American Journal of Public Health* 93; 2003: 1089–97.

6

The Future and Intimate Partner Violence

The first shelters for battered women were opened in the mid-1960s through the early 1970s. Those shelters provided women and children with a place to flee from the abuse they were suffering at home, and represented the first real effort to assist victims of intimate violence. Despite dramatic changes in how such violence is addressed over the years, the overall picture hasn't shifted much in the interim. In the early days of the battered women's movement, an average of three women were murdered every day in the United States by their husbands or boyfriends, or, more often, their ex-husbands or boyfriends. Despite the progress made in understanding the dynamics of abusive relationships and attempts to improve the means to address this crime, we are still, in 2016, losing at least three women a day to domestic violence.[1] Often, entire families are murdered, along with extended family members and bystanders.

We have learned that many intimate partner homicides or homicide/suicides are preventable, and one of the first steps in addressing the problem is the need to listen to victims. After all, they are the ones who have the most complete understanding of what a perpetrator is capable of doing, and time and again, their predictions about their situations come terribly true. In police parlance, they are the chief sources of intelligence. But sadly, too many people in the criminal justice system still discount victims' concerns and label them "hysterical"—until they wind up dead.

Domestic violence is a crime of escalation. The perpetrator's toolbox contains everything from a dozen red roses and the perfect little black dress, to threats, a firearm, a knife or hands around the victim's throat. Perpetrators start their mission to control by being the most charming, attentive, seductive man that the woman has ever encountered. We now know that these tactics are just that—tactics.

They are a part a continuum that shows that the perpetrator is far from being out of control. Quite the contrary: Control is the goal. She does not see it coming, but he is perfectly clear in what he is setting up.

Many people still think intimate partner violence is a crime that touches only certain groups of people (poor, uneducated, people of color), but while lower socioeconomic status is associated with a higher rate of intimate partner violence, we know that women from all socioeconomic groups are victimized. The recent case involving high-powered attorney J. Michael Farren illuminates the stark reality of domestic violence in upper-class families:

J. Michael Farren, a former deputy White House counsel under President George W. Bush and general counsel for Xerox, nearly killed his wife, Mary Margaret Farren, in 2010 after she served him with divorce papers as she tried to escape their abusive marriage. Terrified and isolated, with a very powerful and wealthy perpetrator, Mary Margaret spent 12 years walking on eggshells in an effort to curb her husband's temper. However, on the night of the attack, there was nothing she could do as Farren strangled and bludgeoned her mercilessly with his fists and a flashlight, telling her, "I am killing you." When you live in a 9500 square foot home on a large estate, it's unlikely that anyone will hear you scream.

Mary Margaret fled with her two small children in the couple's BMW and made it to a neighbor's house, where the police and an ambulance were summoned. Photographs of her in the hospital show the grisly results of the assault, with a lacerated face, broken nose and jaw and bruised arms, legs and torso. She leans forward, and the entire chair behind her is black with blood. Her vomiting blood forced the police to stop interviewing her a second time. Police then arrested J. Michael at their home, and Mary Margaret began to deal with the fear of retribution from a very rich and powerful perpetrator. According to Mary Margaret, his \$2 million bail was something he could easily write a check for, and she was in constant fear that he would take her children and run. The judge eventually cut her requested amount in half to \$15 million, which was out of his reach, keeping him in Garner Correctional

Institution.[2] Mary Margaret has bravely spoken out about her abuse in an effort to call attention to the fact that intimate partner violence occurs at all socioeconomic levels.

There are many more cases like the Farren case, but because he is a "well-respected" businessman (and the same would hold true for perpetrators who are doctors, lawyers, police chiefs, professors and the like), no one believed that he was *capable* of being abusive. He doesn't fit the stereotype, and she doesn't either. She was trapped in large part due to his reputation in the community, and this is true of too many women facing intimate partner violence in the United States. These stereotypes are dangerous in this manner, and must be done away with once and for all. Despite an increased risk for those with lower socioeconomic status, no one is immune to domestic violence.

The Violence Against Women Act

When the Violence Against Women Act (VAWA) was passed in 1994, it marked a sea change in how the United States contemplated gender-based and intimate partner violence. The federal government recognized the epidemic of domestic and sexual violence that was affecting one out of every three women, and VAWA set out to address and prevent these crimes. Money was set aside to provide more shelter space for women and children, to train law enforcement officers and prosecutors, and to do much-needed research. Those changes have been vitally important.

Across the country, a scattering of police departments have established divisions dedicated entirely to investigating domestic and sexual violence crimes, and dedicated domestic violence/sexual assault prosecutors have approached their work with a greater degree of thoughtfulness and sophistication regarding the intimate and complex nature of dealing with these crimes in particular. This has led to a greater understanding of the unique aspects of crimes committed by intimate partners rather than strangers.

Intimate partner violence crimes are not black and white; they are crimes that occur in shades of gray. It's relatively easy to want to see a stranger who has harmed or threatened you or a family member prosecuted to the fullest extent of the law, but how does that change when the offender is someone you love and have shared a portion of your life with; had children with; and expected to be with for the rest of your life?

The research that has been done over the last three decades has helped us understand what domestic violence victims are up against. It is never just about the abuser: it is also the systems that still treat crimes against women with a degree of diminished concern. In North Carolina, for example, there is a charge still commonly used in domestic violence prosecutions called *misdemeanor* assault with a deadly weapon. This means that a woman can be shot or stabbed by her abuser, and unless it involves an injury to a vital organ, the crime will be charged at the misdemeanor level. In South Carolina, a state that is usually on the top 10 list for domestic violence homicides (78% of domestic violence homicides in South Carolina committed with firearms), Attorney General Alan Wilson reminds us that a man can receive 5 years for beating his dog but only 30 days for beating his wife. The criminal justice system becomes an echo chamber for both abusers and victims: They *both* know that the assault/s will *not be taken seriously*, so victims drop the charges or refuse to testify because they, better than anyone else, are aware of the short- and long-term consequences of participating in the prosecution process. If he has stabbed her, shot her or beaten her badly, and the courts still regard this assault as nothing more than a misdemeanor-level offense, why should she take the risk of participating? If he has told her that he will kill her if she cooperates, and she is aware of what he has done in the past and (essentially) has gotten away with it, *his word* will become "the law," not the laws on the books in her state. He has abused her and the state has driven the getaway car for him.

However, there are important changes happening. More members of the criminal justice system understand the tactics abusers use to intimidate and control their victims. They understand that he can back her down with one *look*, a look that "tells" her that there will be terrible repercussions for her (and perhaps her family) if she cooperates with law enforcement. Now, many first appearance hearings are done with the abuser in a confined space so that he cannot make eye contact with the victim. This is a huge step in the right direction. For those communities that cannot afford to have a separate area for the abuser, judges, prosecutors and bailiffs can be trained to watch for his intimidating behavior and stop him from doing it. All it requires is being smart about knowing what is happening in the courtroom and establishing clear rules of conduct. (The National Council of Juvenile and Family Court Judges provide training so that judges can sharpen their skills and learn what to look for and how to stop it.)

Lethality Assessment

Dr. Jacquelyn Campbell, a preeminent violence researcher from the Johns-Hopkins School of Nursing, created a very effective and valuable screening tool that first responders can use in the field to determine the relative danger present in each intimate partner violence case.[3] Known for her important contributions to the study of intimate partner violence through methodologically rigorous research, Campbell had determined several factors in domestic violence that led her to develop the assessment. First, only about 4% of victims ever use domestic violence program services, such as hotlines, shelters and advocacy.[4] As such, only a tiny minority are getting the help that is available to them. Second, in more than half of intimate partner homicides, law enforcement officers had previously responded to a call at the scene.[5] This meant that officers had far more chance to help victims than providers, since the victims weren't connecting with the providers except in very rare cases. Finally, research had shown that re-offending against victims who were in great danger was reduced by roughly 60% if they went into a shelter.[6] Campbell saw a clear mandate in these three findings: Women at high risk could be saved if they were hooked up to services, and officers were the ones in the best position to do that, but needed guidance to determine which victims were in greater danger—and thus in greater need of these resources. This led to the creation of the LAP.[7]

When the officer arrives at the scene, he or she assesses the situation. When standards that indicate danger are met, the officer should separate the victim and offender, and ask the victim to answer a series of questions to help determine the risk, and to help the victim understand her risk. The tool developed to explore the situation with the victim is called the lethality assessment questionnaire, which contains ten to fifteen questions designed to gauge specific factors that have been shown to indicate a higher level of risk for lethal violence (see Appendix II for a lethality assessment questionnaire). These questions allow the law enforcement officers to do a quick, risk-informed, assessment in the field, helping them maximize the effectiveness of their response to a particular situation. Perhaps more importantly, the assessment allows the victim to process what has been happening to her, and better understand just how dangerous the relationship has become, increasing the likelihood that she'll reach out for help.

While there are a variety of different procedures that are employed in different jurisdictions, a common one is that officers explain the danger to the victim, and try to initiate a call to a hotline counselor. If the victim chooses not to speak with the counselor, the officer further counsels her to stay vigilant for warning signs, encourages her to contact a domestic violence program and provides her with referral information so she has it should she wish to contact them later. The officer may also discuss safety measures the victim might take.

If the victim chooses to speak with the hotline counselor, the officer responds based on the outcome of that conversation. For example, they might participate in coordinated safety planning with the domestic violence provider and the victim. What is important in either case is that the victim has been given help to connect with services that might save her life, and has been encouraged to take her victimization seriously. An evaluation of a LAP program in Maryland revealed another benefit of the protocol: Officers reported that using the tool was an eye-opener for them in terms of gaining a better understanding of the danger inherent in intimate partner violence. The vast majority of officers also reported that they appreciated the tool, and that it helped them do their jobs better.[8] In terms of connecting victims with services, other procedures grew out of LAP that further increased gains. Many jurisdictions have started following up with victims determined to be at the greatest risk either by phone or in a home visit (with an officer and advocate) soon after the incident, and have realized amazing improvement in victims using services.[9]

Another avenue for improvement is found in the protective order process. In some jurisdictions, deputies conduct lethality assessments with victims immediately following temporary and interim order of protection meetings. Where victims are determined to be at high risk, deputies or advocates speak with the victim about the dangerous nature of their situations and their options for help.[10] This provides another front on which to address the problem.

Lethality Assessment Programs (LAPs) continue to evolve in response to research on their effectiveness, which has brought about many improvements. In 2009, states using the LAP started using guidelines to help train hotline counselors to respond more efficiently and effectively when officers initiate calls from crime scenes. These communications are different from calls under other circumstances in that time on the phone is shorter, and victims aren't as prepared to speak with a counselor as when they initiate the call themselves after some thought. These guidelines standardize and streamline the discussion with the victim to maximize the likelihood that she will seek help.[11]

One last positive feature of LAP is that the experience and gut instincts of law enforcement officers are not discarded in this approach. The program suggests that the assessment tool should be employed when an officer senses that there is a "manifestation of danger" through any of the following means:

1. The officer believes that an assault or other violent act has occurred, whether or not there was probable cause for arrest.
2. The officer is concerned for the victim-survivor's safety once they leave the incident scene.
3. The officer is responding to a domestic violence call from a victim-survivor or at a location where intimate partner violence has occurred in the past.
4. The officer has a gut feeling that the victim-survivor is in danger.[12]

Overall, evaluation research results are showing definite gains in the safety of victims through the use of LAPs.[13] Discussing the situation in the relationship with someone (an advocate, law enforcement officer or both) helps victims start developing a plan of action, even if they are too shocked or scared to do it during the time officers are on the scene. It also gets them connected to resources and a support system without having to do the legwork themselves. A final benefit of lethality assessment is that friends and family members can assist a victim of intimate partner violence complete it, as well as that it provides a useful tool for anyone seeking to help.

Offender Treatment Programs

By 1991, every state in the country had adopted court-mandated treatment programs for intimate partner violence offenders known as Spouse Abuse Abatement Programs (SAAPs) or, more commonly, Batterer Intervention Programs (BIPs).[14] Most advocates started out with great hope that these programs would prove successful, especially as they shift the focus from victims to offenders in addressing the violence. Unfortunately, there is nearly a consensus in the research—a very rare occurrence in the social sciences—that these programs show a very limited, if any, impact on reducing the violent behavior of offenders.[15]

Typical findings show offenders' attitudes and behavior are not significantly different after participating in treatment than perpetrators who did not undergo treatment.[16] Worse, there are a number of negative unintended consequences that result from these programs. For example, research shows that women are far more likely to reconcile with partners who have undergone treatment due to a false sense of security that the offender has been rehabilitated, which might put her in danger of future violence.[17] Perhaps more importantly, scarce funds to address the problem of intimate partner violence are channelled into these programs that produce little in the way of progress, when that money is likely better spent in other areas that would yield better results in keeping victims safe.[18]

Some researchers and clinical practitioners believe that it would be premature to give up on BIPs, primarily because they believe that there might be more effective ways to administer these programs, such as focusing on certain types of offenders, addressing concurrent issues such as drug or alcohol abuse, posttraumatic stress disorder (PTSD), borderline personality disorder or tailoring these programs to specific ethnic groups, but to date, evaluation research hasn't confirmed whether these efforts to specialize improve results.[19] These programs can be costly, and even in jurisdictions where the offender foots the bill, it is likely that the victim feels the financial bite of this cost, as well. In a national survey, most judges reported ordering treatment as a form of accountability (75%) or rehabilitation (90%).[20] Accountability actually does have an impact on reoffending—but there are more direct ways to meet that goal. Overall, despite the fact that they are well-intentioned and in wide use, these programs are an example of something that sounds great, but doesn't actually have much of an effect in practice.

A Possible Exception: The Beit Noam Residential Program for Men

Perhaps the most innovative and comprehensive program to address and end domestic violence was launched in Tel Aviv, Israel, in 1997, and unlike most other treatment programs for offenders, this one shows great promise. Beit Noam, a residential treatment program for men, was developed when advocates, scholars and activists who worked with battered women and their abusers looked at domestic violence through an entirely different lens. They decided that forcing women and children to flee and hide in a battered women's shelter was a form of revictimization that sent the wrong message to everyone involved. Rather than forcing women and children to reconfigure their lives and leave behind everything they know, including their homes, friends, pets, schools and jobs, why not build a facility where abusers are sent? After all, shelters are very much like domestic violence refugee centers, no matter how hard advocates work to make them as comfortable as possible, victims should not be the ones forced to relocate to shelters.

The Beit Noam Residential Program for Violent Men was founded as a live-in intervention program for abusive men focusing on "combating the core of the phenomena of intimate violence. The main goals of treating male batterers are to: (1) allow battered women and their children to remain in their homes and in their natural environment; (2) treat, re-socialize and teach self-controlling skills and normative behaviors to the male batterers; and (3) stop the pattern of intimate violence being transferred across generations."[21]

This is a bold new way to rethink the crime of domestic violence. Shelters are still a central and important part of providing holistic services for women and children fleeing abusive partners, but if we remain committed to *requiring* women and children to run and hide, we will continue to send a message to the abuser that his victims will be the ones inconvenienced by his abuse. We do not do this with any other kind of criminal conduct. (We do not, for example, tell a bank president to move his branch after it has been repeatedly robbed; law enforcement officers know bank robbery is a crime, and they treat it as such, focusing their efforts on catching and punishing the offenders. Asking a bank president to flee would seem ludicrous.)

At Beit Noam, as in BIPs in the United States, the focus is placed directly on the offender. However, the guiding principles at Beit Noam are different from nonresidential programs in that they operate on these assumptions:

1. It is important to treat the root behavior of the domestic violence problem, which is the behavior of the violent man.
2. It is important to ban the assailant from his home and offer the victims—his wife and children—a chance to live without terror and fear.
3. It is essential to stop the intergenerational transmission of domestic violence.
4. There is a good chance of eliminating violence behavior among treatable men through their residence in an open housing setting that offers an integrated, intensive framework for intervention and education with the support of the law.[22]

Like abuser treatment programs in the United States, Beit Noam focuses on getting the abusive man to take responsibility for his choice to be abusive and controlling. Through various therapeutic approaches, including a 4-month residential stay, he is taught to understand that he is responsible for his behavior at all times, and that his violence is not the fault of his partner (or anyone else he might seek to blame).[23] However, the facilitators at Beit Noam recognize that many men who are abusive were exposed to violence as children, so childhood exposure is addressed in both group and individual therapy.[24]

Another feature of Beit Noam that seems to be of great value is the group living setting with other men who are abusive. Having other men at various stages of dealing with their abusive behavior in close proximity allows men to learn from other violent men who are trying to change. Additionally, through sharing living space with other men, they learn to express their thoughts and feelings in a constructive, nonviolent way, while learning to respect the positions of others. This prepares them for reintegration into their families.

Through an integrative therapeutic model combining cognitive, psychodynamic and educational approaches, residents "learn to recognize the preliminary signs of a violent event and develop strategies for self-control with the aim of eliminating his aggressive reaction."[25] The men who are admitted to the Beit Noam program are considered relatively hard-core abusers, and interviews with their partners sheds light on both the severity and tactics the offender employed. After the 4-month stay at Beit Noam, parole officers' reports showed "not one of the men who had completed 4 months of therapy at Beit Noam returned to wife or child abuse during a period of more than a year after completion of therapy."[26]

The program's therapists do not believe the offenders are completely reformed by any means, but it has been shown that, with continued therapy once they have rejoined their families (or divorced and moved into new relationships), the level of abusive and controlling behavior is significantly diminished. The Beit Noam Model provides a highly structured, multilevel therapeutic experience that packs a triple punch of accountability, responsibility and hope.

Focused Deterrence Programs: The Example of High Point, North Carolina

In High Point, North Carolina, the police department, in conjunction with area domestic violence and other community-based programs, decided to collaborate with David Kennedy, director of the Center for Crime Prevention and Control at John Jay College of Criminal Justice in New York, to develop and implement an offender focused domestic violence initiative (OFDVI) for intimate partner perpetrators. Kennedy's approach rests on the premise that not enough attention is paid to controlling the offender.[27] Focused deterrence had been shown effective in controlling gang and drug-related violence, and the High Point police department wanted to see if the same approach would work with domestic violence offenders.[28]

The focus of the program was based on the following premise: "Traditional approaches have been victim-focused with heavy emphasis on helping the victim to avoid patterns of abuse and physically removing themselves from abusive settings. What if in addition to providing services to the victim we used very focused formal and informal sanctions against the offender? Can the domestic violence offender be held accountable with real predictable consequences? These are the questions the partnership in High Point has set out to answer."[29] One of the key features of the program is an emphasis on dealing with offenders at earlier stages of offending, before the violence escalates and the secrecy is entrenched.[30] Research suggests that early intervention is a key factor in ending the cycle of intimate partner violence.[31] The goals for the initiative were to (1) protect the most vulnerable women from the most dangerous perpetrators, (2) remove the burden of dealing with abusers from the victim and place it on the police, (3) focus police deterrence, community standards, support and outreach on the most dangerous offenders, (4) avoid the "experiential effect" of perpetrators, where they learn the wrong lessons from the experience of other offenders, (5) exploit opportunities derived from the variety of an offender's offenses, and (6) avoid putting victims at additional risk.[32]

This is a bold and appropriate way to rethink the crime of domestic violence. While shelters remain a central and important part of providing holistic services for women and children fleeing abusive situations, if we remain committed to requiring women and children to run and hide, we will continue to send a message to the abuser that his victims will be the ones inconvenienced by his abuse. We do not take this approach with any other kind of criminal conduct, and it needs to change in the case of intimate partner violence. In the first 2 years of the program, the initiative resulted in a 9% recidivism rate. Given that the average rate of re-offending across the domestic violence literature is 20%–30%, this is an amazing reduction.[33]

Even more impressive news came in the form of intimate partner homicide prevention: From 2004 to 2008, 17 homicides in High Point involved intimate partners. The program was implemented in 2009, and in all the years since OFDVI, there has been one murder attributed to an intimate partner in High Point.[34] Moreover, this is a smart policing strategy in terms of resources: Addressing intimate partner violence accounts for one of the biggest drains on departmental assets (think about the high volume of calls, repeated calls to the same location, a marked investment in time and, of course, the significant number of injuries and deaths). As we see in the example from High Point, offender-focused strategies have great potential.

Trauma-Informed Advocacy

The concept of trauma-informed advocacy has been around for a while, but is relatively new as a formal model for use in helping survivors of intimate partner violence. Domestic violence advocates have always known that one of the single most important aspects of providing supportive services for victims who have experienced abuse starts with listening to them and reinforcing that their circumstances were traumatic and undeserved, but trauma-informed advocacy provides more specific guidelines to use in addressing the emotional needs of victims.[35] Each woman has her own unique history. For some, the abuse they are currently experiencing is the most recent in a long history of abuse. For others, the relationship they now find themselves trapped in is unlike anything they have ever experienced before. For all survivors, the thoughts and feelings associated with the abuse are complex and confusing, and the emotional consequences are profound.

In cases where the victim knew their offender prior to the criminal act, there is an additional layer of fear, confusion and betrayal that tends to worsen as the intimacy in the relationship increases. As such, violence at the hands of an intimate partner creates additional emotional damage, as the victim doubts their own judgment, along with their self-worth.[36] Feelings of shame, guilt and isolation are common, as are shock, terror, disbelief, confusion and despair.[37] Victims are also very likely to experience a variety of psychiatric symptoms, including hyperarousal, anxiety, sleep disruption, avoidance of reminders and reliving the traumatic event.[38]

PTSD and clinical depression are very common, and research has shown that survivors are likely to have experienced cumulative trauma from other events, such as childhood abuse, as well.[39] One of several difficulties in addressing PTSD in victims of intimate partner violence is that most treatments developed to address the disorder were developed to help patients recover from *past* trauma—such as combat or sexual assault—but domestic violence survivors are often dealing with ongoing threats, no matter their relationship status (since estranged partners can be an even greater danger to them).[40] As such, many symptoms associated with PTSD, such as a heightened sense of fear, are a rational response to a continued threat rather than a disordered reaction to memories of past violence. This makes many therapeutic procedures employed in treating PTSD ineffective, or even harmful in some cases.[41] More universal problems in victims seeking therapy include difficulties in affording treatment, child care issues, more pressing concerns such as safety and the needs of children, and a lack of energy and motivation to make necessary arrangements due to the effects of depression.[42] When these issues are addressed and victims do receive therapy, the trauma-focused treatments that show the greatest effectiveness across a variety of populations are cognitive therapy (CT) and cognitive behavioral therapy (CBT).[43]

Trauma-informed advocacy focuses on both the emotional and the physical safety of the survivor, and there are five core components to trauma-informed advocacy initiatives that facilitate this goal:

1. Providing survivors with comprehensive and situation-specific information about the traumatizing effects of all types of abuse.
2. Adapting programs to meet survivors' complex trauma and mental health-related needs.
3. Creating opportunities for the survivor to openly examine their responses and reactions to their trauma without judgment.
4. Making sure survivors have access to all necessary resources and referrals, including resources for the children.
5. Remaining mindful of our own responses and how our program's services appropriately meet the needs of survivors.[44]

It is essential to provide the safe and respectful space that survivors need to take steps to ensure their safety and begin the process of healing. A real understanding of what victims are going through is crucial in helping them escape the violence for anyone, from law enforcement, to friends and family, to advocates, to court personnel and attorneys.[45] Trauma-informed advocacy brings a structured awareness of the emotional hurdles facing survivors, and thus is something of a no-brainer in meeting their needs.

Mandatory Arrest: The Legacy of the Minneapolis Experiment

You will likely be familiar with the 1981 Minneapolis experiment on the impact of arrest in police calls for assistance with intimate partner violence. It spurred the creation of most mandatory and preferred arrest policies in the United States due to its most noteworthy finding: that offenders who were arrested for their assaults—rather than counselled or temporarily separated—were far less likely to reoffend against their victims during a 6-month follow-up period.[46] This research sparked a sea change in police response to domestic violence, which was too often treated as a private, family matter by the criminal justice system at the time, resulting in mostly noninterventionist approaches from law enforcement.[47] At the time, advocates were frustrated by the lack of legal intervention from police, and successfully sued several police departments for failing to make arrests in very serious cases that ended in homicides.[48]

In the wake of Larry Sherman's Minneapolis experiment, police policy around the country started to shift almost overnight toward arresting offenders, and in many cases, toward the mandatory arrest of offenders. This shift was huge: Estimates vary due to variations in policies, but the number of police departments with some type of pro-arrest policy in place jumped from roughly 10% before the study to roughly 46% by 1986.[49] In many places where this dictate is not official, there are still de facto mandatory arrest policies in place; grants designed to encourage arrest, the widespread belief that mandatory arrest works, and countless hours of police training have seen to this.[50] While the results of this paradigm shift in policing are not all positive, it is important to remember that every policy has unintended negative consequences, and that the move toward criminalization of these offenders was necessary at the time in beginning to respond to intimate partner violence as a serious, violent crime that warranted formal intervention.

Replications of the Minneapolis experiment have shown a variety of results, some of which do not support mandatory arrest policies.[51] However, a meta-analysis of four National Institute of Justice (NIJ)-sponsored replications using consistent methodology produced a 25% reduction in recidivism rates with arrest.[52] While it's true that the methodology in many of these studies varied from the original experiment in many cases, this doesn't mean the later results were invalid—only that they cannot be used to question the results of the original study, since they were not obtained in the same manner. However, due to the variety of results obtained in subsequent research, questions certainly persist about whether mandatory arrest is the panacea that Sherman and his colleagues suggested.

The police certainly needed to take intimate violence more seriously at the time, and there needed to be consequences for offenders (as with any other type of crime). It's possible that mandatory policies were necessary to make that shift initially, but that victims might be better served by a slightly different tact now. Removing the logic and common sense of law enforcement officers is rarely a good idea, as we saw in the case of mandatory sentencing schemes, with their goal of removing discretion from judges. Such policies tend to create more problems than they solve in creating one response for a variety of situations. One size rarely fits all.

Advocates make valid arguments that the criminal justice system often ignores the complex needs of victims, and the context of the violence against them. In the case of law enforcement, mandatory arrest policies *dictate* that officers cannot take these factors into consideration through attempting to eliminate officer discretion, and one consequence of this is that family conflict (or normal couple violence) often must be treated as intimate partner violence, resulting in arrests that are inappropriate. Such situations likely have additional detrimental effects through blurring the line between domestic squabbles and abuse, and decreasing officers' respect for arrest as an appropriate option in situations where intimate partner violence is a form of victimization.[53]

Another issue arises in determining who the primary aggressor is in domestic violence situations; though most police now receive training to make this determination, it is a difficult call in many situations, especially where the victim has used physical self-defense. Many have theorized that dual arrest is resulting in many arrests of victims of intimate partner violence, which is a source of secondary victimization as well as a deterrent to calling the police for help. However understandable those fears are, a nationwide study of arrest in intimate partner violence cases showed that dual arrest is rarely employed, so the impact on victims is negligible at best (in fact, dual arrest was only employed in 1.9% of calls).[54] It is difficult to imagine that dual arrest is always unwarranted, so this rate suggests that there might be less of a problem than many people imagine. However, there are certainly jurisdictions where inappropriate use of dual arrest is a problem, but it is one that is easily addressed: Research has demonstrated that departments with primary aggressor policies or laws, which state that officers should identify and arrest only the main offender in an incident, report one-fourth the number of dual arrests compared to jurisdictions without such policies or laws in place.[55] Officers seem to appreciate these policies and laws, as well.

Other issues and criticisms with respect to mandatory arrest in the case of intimate partner offenders further muddy the waters. For example, there has been repeated criticism over the years that the 6-month follow-up period in the Minneapolis research was too short to accurately measure recidivism due to the episodic and cyclical of violence seen in domestic violence situations. As such, many perpetrators might not have offended again during that window with or without police intervention, and may well have offended again after that period.[56] Another point of concern with mandatory arrest is that it may hurt victims in some cases. The Minneapolis experiment was based on deterrence theory—the idea being that offenders would desist from offending if they feared arrest—but some offenders might not be engaging in such rational decision making. In these cases, the offender might retaliate violently against their victim for their arrest. Given the number of murder-suicides that occur in the context of intimate partner violence, it is clear that some offenders are as likely to be provoked as deterred. Moreover, it is important to remember that removing the victim's wishes from the equation is a double-edged sword: While the victim is relieved of the scary responsibility of pressing charges against the offender, she is also relieved of her choice in the matter, which might make some victims reluctant to seek help from police.

Overall, there is evidence that preferred arrest laws might be more effective than mandatory arrest laws, while allowing victims and law enforcement officers more discretion in addressing situations where there are complicated factors at play. Mandatory arrest laws increase the likelihood of dual arrests occurring, and actually result in fewer arrests than preferred arrest laws. Nationally, arrest rates in jurisdictions with mandatory arrest laws were 97% higher than in jurisdictions with discretionary arrest laws, but were a whopping 177% higher in jurisdictions with preferred arrest laws in place.[57] These findings indicate that we still need policies to promote arrest to protect victims and hold offenders accountable, but that allowing officers and victims some discretion might prove more beneficial, and reduce some of the unintended negative consequences of mandatory arrest as we move forward.

Global Positioning System Tracking

One very unique feature of ongoing domestic violence is that it is one crime where we actually know who the victim will be ahead of time, which should make violence prevention far easier. Global positioning system (GPS) tracking is a promising new approach to enhancing the safety of intimate partner violence victims that takes advantage of this fact. Early evaluations are showing positive outcomes in both enforcing court mandated orders for no contact and for use as a form of pretrial supervision. GPS use in intimate partner violence cases has been increasing since the mid-1990s, with 23 states currently using the technology in this manner for high-risk domestic violence offenders, and 11 more have pending legislation to adopt its use.[58]

Since 2004, Connecticut has had GPS tracking in place for high-risk offenders, and in the areas where the program is in place, there hasn't been a single intimate partner homicide in the 11 years since the program was instituted.[59] Similarly, promising results have been found in larger, scientific studies of GPS use in domestic violence. Compared with regular supervision, as well as radio frequency (RF) monitoring, which remotely monitors defendants under house arrest without tracking capabilities, GPS tracking resulted in both short- and long-term gains in compliance with program rules, and, more importantly, resulted in practically no contact attempts.[60] Further, there were long-term gains in reducing recidivism for both intimate partner violence and other offenses.[61] Surprisingly, in qualitative interviews, perpetrators even noted several benefits of GPS tracking, including protection against false accusations, making it easier for them to envision a future without the victim, and added structure in their lives.[62] An important caveat from the researchers addresses implementation of GPS programs for domestic violence:

> Policy implications highlight the importance of having a logical connection between defendant attributes and program details, avoiding enrollment in cases where the GPS has minimal or no value and is imposed for reasons other than protecting victims or enforcing restraining orders, the need for justice professionals to cultivate relationships with victims whose abusers are on GPS, and the importance of maintaining an appropriate balance between victim safety and due process for the defendant.[63]

Some argue that the use of GPS tracking is cost prohibitive. The National Institute of Justice noted that monitoring sex offenders with GPS costs roughly $36 a day per offender, with traditional supervision costing $27/day.[64] The cost differential would be roughly the same for intimate partner perpetrators, and given the impressive results in keeping victims safe, the additional expense seems like a solid expenditure. However, with budgets as they are in most states, it will require making such action a priority, and training and education about the benefits are often required to make judges and law enforcement see the value in this approach. Stalking is a far too common feature of intimate partner violence, particularly where the offender is estranged from the victim, and GPS tracking is often the only way that victims can prove they are being stalked.[65]

The ACLU has taken exception to the use of GPS tracking in the case of sex offenders, and will likely do so in the case of domestic violence offenders, as well. Their complaint is that the device has been used on offenders who were convicted prior to the enactment of GPS tracking laws, that some of the offenders in the program are not high risk, that the devices are heavy and uncomfortable, produce stigma when visible, and that some states require the offenders to pay for the service.[66] Certainly, this technology should only be used with higher-risk offenders, and we won't delve into the legal issues of retroactively applying this legislation, but where an offender presents a clear threat to the safety of his ex-intimate partner, a bit of discomfort and expense seem like a fair tradeoff. In fact, isn't it more appropriate that the offender bears the discomfort and expense than the victim? She is often compelled to install alarms, new locks and the like, and it is certainly uncomfortable to be terrorized by a violent offender. Perhaps the burden is fairly placed on the perpetrator of the violence, who has earned the inconvenience.

Domestic Violence Courts

During the 1990s, many jurisdictions created domestic violence courts to aid victims, hold offenders accountable, deliver more consistent rulings on intimate partner violence statutes, and better ensure follow-through on cases. Most of these courts also place a greater emphasis on deterrence and rehabilitation of offenders.[67] Greater judicial involvement and continuity is a key feature in these courts, which appears to facilitate court knowledge of noncompliance on the part of the offender (such as orders of protection, probation requirements and the like), leading to the imposition of penalties for infractions.[68] This simultaneously holds the offender to a higher degree of responsibility, while keeping victims safer.

Ideally, the court has significant contact with the offender, though this isn't always the case in practice: A nationwide evaluation showed that the domestic violence courts with the most intensive judicial monitoring had offenders appearing twice a month, with the least only four times a year.[69] Similar disparities in practices are found in whether the courts order batterer treatment, with about half reporting that they order treatment often or always, but more than 40% doing so rarely or never.[70] At their best, domestic violence courts provide a number of services to facilitate victim comfort and involvement in the court process, such as offering counseling, child care, safety escorts and safety planning at the courthouse, but most fall short of this level of service.[71] Naturally, good planning and the availability of resources tend to determine the level of services particular courts are able to offer. Court workers consistently viewed a lack of time and resources as the biggest barrier to victim involvement in the process.

Researchers have identified frequent judicial monitoring of offenders and dedicated victim advocates for victims as having an important role in achieving the goals of offender accountability and victim safety, so scarce resources should be directed to these pursuits to maximize the benefits of domestic violence courts. Judges in these courts walk a fine line in order to be most effective. It is important that they be perceived as not unduly biased toward the victim, though research has consistently shown that domestic violence court judges do not give excessive punishments to offenders.[72] Another characteristic of a good domestic violence court judge is empathy. A key feature that aids in the development of this trait is having judges dedicated to presiding over cases from arraignment through disposition. In this manner, the judge gets to know the history and dynamics of a particular intimate partner violence situation, which increases consistency and understanding.[73]

Evaluation efforts are starting to yield results, most of which show a positive impact on conviction rates and victim satisfaction with the judicial process.[74] Future research will undoubtedly improve these innovations through honing the important factors in the success of these courts. Overall, domestic violence courts hold great promise in increasing victim safety and increasing offender accountability for their violent crimes.

The Duluth Model: Coordinated Community Response

The Duluth Model harnesses community and criminal justice resources in a coordinated response to increase victim safety and offender accountability. Law enforcement, advocacy groups, local courts, probation programs, treatment programs and battered women's shelters work together to end domestic violence. Communities using the coordinated community response (CCR) approach:

- Take the blame off the victim and placed the accountability for abuse on the offender.
- Share policies and procedures for holding offenders accountable and keeping victims safe across all agencies in the criminal and civil justice systems from 911 to the courts.
- Prioritize the voices and experiences of women who experience battering in the creation of those policies and procedures.
- Believe that battering is a pattern of actions used to intentionally control or dominate an intimate partner and actively

works to change societal conditions that support men's use of tactics of power and control over women.
- Offer change opportunities for offenders through court-ordered educational groups for batterers.
- Have ongoing discussions between criminal and civil justice agencies, community members and victims to close gaps and improve the community's response to battering.[75]

One of the key features of the Duluth Model is that it is grounded in the experience of victims, drawing from their unique understanding of dealing with intimate partner violence. This input is essential in avoiding the unintended negative consequences that often arise in initiatives that are developed without consulting victims. For example, one of the directives from victims was that they wanted their abusers to receive treatment in order to keep them from reoffending, thus making them safer. In response to this, the Duluth Model incorporates nonviolence courses designed to help offenders look more closely at their behavior, beliefs, intentions and the effects of their actions on the victim and others.[76]

However, research suggests less than stellar outcomes with the use of CCR, though the biggest weakness appears to lie in the batterer treatment program aspect of the initiative.[77]

Critics of CCR charge that the model ignores research linking domestic violence to substance abuse and psychological disorders such as attachment disorders, which are often linked to childhood abuse and neglect.[78] In fairness, the Duluth Model is more than treatment for batterers, and much of the research judging it as having little to no effect on outcomes focuses on this one aspect of the model, and often judges the Duluth Model as having failed when they are not evaluating the other aspects of the initiative.[79] As we've already seen, the vast majority of research on BIPs shows that they are not very, if at all, effective.[80] This is depressing news, since it is one of the few interventions that are directed toward requiring action on the part of offenders rather than victims.

Coordinating criminal justice and community response to intimate partner violence is necessary in order to maximize the effectiveness of both avenues for intervention in intimate violence, and we've seen success in other areas where these connections are formed, such as

LAPs and court advocacy. As such, we believe that the benefits of CCR will likely be borne out through more careful and comprehensive evaluation research.

Addressing Unhealthy Masculinity

The final response to intimate partner violence that we want to address is centered on men, and though there is little research on its efficacy, this type of program has the potential to make drastic changes in the relationship between males and violence. It is an effort to change the culture of masculinity that seems very promising, and, at the very least, will likely result in a culture that features more men who would not perpetrate violence against women (and others), and that allows men more freedom from restrictive gender roles. In his highly acclaimed TED Talk, Tony Porter, co-creator of the domestic violence prevention program, *A Call to Men*, with Ted Bunch, presents what he calls the "man box"—which contains the behavior men must adhere to in order to act the part of a man. The box contains the following rules and roles:

1. Don't cry or openly express emotions—with the exception of anger
2. Don't show weakness or fear
3. Demonstrate power and control—especially over women
4. Aggression and dominance
5. Protector
6. Don't be "like a woman"
7. Heterosexual—don't be "like a gay man"
8. Be tough, athletic, strong and courageous
9. Make decisions—don't need help
10. View women as property/objects[81]

Porter points out that these proscriptions for masculinity not only lead men to disrespect, abuse and mistreat women, but also one another. He tells the story of asking a male athlete what his reaction would be if his coach said he was playing like a girl in front of his teammates. Porter expected to hear an answer such as "embarrassed" or "angry," but was really struck by the answer he received: The young man said he would be "destroyed."[82] Porter makes an excellent point in noting how inferior men must view women for this to be the case.

A Call to Men is a program designed to help men break out of the "man box," and some of the suggestions for doing so give a good idea about the nature of the program (and others like it). They include:

- Learn how well-intentioned men can stand up and speak out against violence.
- Take on violence against women and girls as a human rights issue: Write a letter to the editor about women's rights, participate in a domestic violence or sexual assault prevention event, organize a fundraiser and send the donations to a women's rights organization.
- Challenge comments that tease or harass men and boys for not being "manly" enough. Let people know that you find it offensive and limiting.
- Talk with men and boys in your life about healthy manhood and the importance of respecting women and girls.
- Express your broad range of emotions—including fear, sadness and hurt—and support other men and boys in expressing their emotions in a safe way.
- Challenge yourself and others not to use language or expressions that denigrate women and girls (such as "you throw like a girl" or "man up").
- Give equal affection to your sons and your daughters. Demonstrate to them that healthy manhood involves hugging, holding hands and kindness.[83]

Given the vast disparity in rates of violent offending between men and women, there is good reason to believe that the great differences in the way boys and girls are socialized plays a role, and there has been a significant amount of research on this relationship.[84] Like many of these programs, the Mentors in Violence Prevention (MVP) Project at Northeastern University seeks to inspire athletes and other men who are viewed as successful in traditional masculinity to use their stature on campus to promote healthier attitudes and behaviors toward women.[85]

In Texas, the Men's Nonviolence Project focuses mostly on educating men and boys about masculinity, privilege and getting involved as allies to reduce violence against women and girls.[86] There are many people out there doing this work with an eye toward changing this dynamic in the future. These programs are based on the most fundamental goal of feminism: that men and women should be treated equally, and should have the same opportunities. While the obvious goal is to address violence against women, these initiatives also actively seek to improve the lives of men through freeing them from the limitations of traditional masculine roles.[87]

Many social problems require a paradigm shift in culture to address, and to some, this might seem like a daunting, if not impossible, task. However, there are numerous examples of paradigm shifts in culture that would have seemed far less likely to have occurred than men taking on fuller roles than "real men" are currently able to do. For example, if someone had asked you even 10 years ago if marriage equality for gays and lesbians would be the law of the land, you likely would have guessed that would never happen due to entrenched attitudes and prejudices against this group. However, this represents a paradigm shift in the culture. Similarly, women's roles and notions of femininity have changed dramatically, though over a longer period of time. Why couldn't our ideas about men and notions of masculinity change? There has already been some change, which is more evident in younger men because of different ideas already present in raising boys. For example, it is pretty normal and acceptable for young people to split the bill on a date these days, rather than having the assumption be that the man should have to pay for everything (How is that fair? Why should men be the ones to have to pay?). Young men are asked out on dates more often than in the past (and again, why should men have to be the ones to put themselves out there for possible rejection exclusively?). Men are perfectly capable of changing, and good men are perfectly capable of standing up for themselves and others when situations call for it. That's real strength and courage, and hopefully, encouraging men in this direction will result in a future that is far less violent for everyone.

What You Can Do

- Do your best to inform people about the prevalence and seriousness of intimate partner violence.

- Emphasize the difference between common couple violence and domestic violence. While no violence in relationships is optimal, of course, intimate partner violence is dangerous to an extent that common couple violence is not, and there are key differences in roles. People conflating the two likely exacerbate the problem of people minimizing the consequences of domestic violence.
- Write editorials, write your legislators, and generally do everything you can to raise awareness about intimate partner violence.
- Help create options that put the burden on offenders rather than victims. If you can create or support residential programs for perpetrators, do so.
- Help men and boys free themselves from the man box. Start a program to address unhealthy masculinity in your area, or encourage others to do so. Be as mindful of the messages you send about expectations for men as you are for women.
- Spread the word about the importance of lethality assessment, and use it yourself to help victims gain vital perspective on their situations. If the victim is not able to leave immediately, be sure to use the safety planning tool described in Appendix III to help keep her as safe as possible until she can get out.

Discussion Ideas

1. Discuss the role of guns in intimate partner violence, and what we could do to make victims safer. Do guns in the home increase or decrease the safety of victims, children and others? Can you think of legal ways to decrease the risk of gun-related homicides occurring?
2. What do you think about the simple idea of requiring perpetrators to leave the home rather than victims and children? Can that work in the United States? What would need to happen? Why do you think more people haven't thought of this idea?
3. Should intimate partner violence be a greater priority for funding and criminal justice training? What do court

room work groups—prosecuting attorneys, judges and the like—need to be doing differently? Law enforcement?

4. Do you have programs to address battering in your area? Are there enough of them? Have they been assessed for their efficacy? Find out how often and when such treatment is required by the courts. Is it often enough, and are the placements appropriate?
5. What can we do to reduce the stigma attached to intimate partner violence? Why is there a stigma to begin with?
6. Discuss the concept of the man box. What are the underlying ideas and messages contained in it? How does it impact men and boys? How does it impact women and girls? Is it healthy? Aside from violence, what negative consequences does it bring for men and women?

References and Notes

1. American Psychological Association, *Intimate Partner Violence: Facts and Resources*, 2015, http://www.apa.org/topics/violence/partner.aspx?item=2 (accessed July 8, 2015).
2. K. Vick, Case of Michael Farren seen as refresher course on domestic violence, *Washington Post*, February 25, 2010, http://www.washingtonpost.com/wp-dyn/content/article/2010/02/24/AR2010022405384.html (accessed January 3, 2015).
3. J. C. Campbell et al., Assessing risk factors for intimate partner homicide, *NIJ Journal* 250; 2002: 14–9; J. C. Campbell, D. Webster, J. Koziol-McLain et al., Risk factors for femicide in abusive relationships: Results from a multisite case control study, *American Journal of Public Health* 93; 2003: 1089–97; J. T. Messing, J. C. Campbell, J. S. Wilson, S. Brown, B. Patchell, and C. Shall, *Police Departments' Use of the Lethality Assessment Program: A Quasi-Experimental Evaluation* (Washington, DC: U.S. Department of Justice, 2014).
4. J. C. Campbell et al., Assessing risk factors in intimate partner homicide, *NIJ Journal* 250; 2002: 14–9.
5. Ibid.
6. Ibid.
7. J. C. Campbell, D. Webster, J. Koziol-McLain et al., Risk factors for femicide in abusive relationships: Results from a multisite case control study, *American Journal of Public Health* 93; 2003: 1089–97.
8. Maryland Network Against Domestic Violence, *Lethality Assessment Program Maryland Model for First Responders: Learning to Read the Danger Signs* (Bowie, MD: Maryland Network Against Domestic

Violence, 2014), http://www.ncdsv.org/images/MNADV_LAPMDModelForFirstRespondersLearningToReadTheDangerSigns.pdf (accessed October 9, 2015). Maryland is considered the model LAP in the United States.

9. In Maryland, for example, in 2008, programs that conducted follow-ups doubled the state average for victims taking advantage of services such as shelters—from 28% to 56%. *Maryland Model for First Responders: Learning to Read the Danger Signs* (Bowie, MD: Maryland Network Against Domestic Violence, 2014), http://www.ncdsv.org/images/MNADV_LAPMDModelForFirstRespondersLearningToReadTheDangerSigns.pdf (accessed October 9, 2015).
10. Using Maryland as an example again, in the period between January 2008 and March of 2009, 37% of the pool of 273 victims who spoke with a hotline counselor or advocate through the protective order process went into domestic violence programs. *Maryland Model for First Responders: Learning to Read the Danger Signs* (Bowie, MD: Maryland Network Against Domestic Violence, 2014), http://www.ncdsv.org/images/MNADV_LAPMDModelForFirstRespondersLearningToReadTheDangerSigns.pdf (accessed October 9, 2015).
11. Ibid.
12. National Institute of Justice, *A Closer Look at the Lethality Assessment Programs* (Washington, DC: National Institute of Justice, 2015), http://www.nij.gov/journals/275/Pages/closer-look-lap.aspx (accessed October 10, 2015); J. T. Messing, J. C. Campbell, and J. S. Wilson, Research designs in the real world: Testing the effectiveness of an IPV intervention, *NIJ Journal* 275; 2015: 1–9.
13. For example, the Kansas City Police Department conducted 8969 lethality screens between June 2009 and June 2013. Of these assessments, 72% of victims were determined to be in the high risk category, and, of those at high risk, roughly half spoke with a hotline counselor. Prior to the initiation of LAP, only 2% of hotline callers reported law enforcement as the source of their referral. Further, in 2012, LAP-initiated referrals accounted for 23% of the 1616 hotline calls—according to their partnering domestic violence service, this represented a 56% increase in the number of LAP-initiated hotline calls from 2010 to 2012. P. 12 Virginia Department of Criminal Justice Services, *Review of Lethality Assessment Programs* (Springfield, VA: Department of Criminal Justice Services, 2013), http://www.postandcourier.com/tilldeath/assets/d1-25.pdf (accessed October 8, 2015). See also J. T. Messing, J. C. Campbell, J. S. Wilson, S. Brown, B. Patchell, and C. Shall, *Police Departments' Use of the Lethality Assessment Program: A Quasi-Experimental Evaluation* (Washington, DC: U.S. Department of Justice, 2014); L. Bennett, L. Goodman, and M. A. Dutton, Risk assessment among batterers arrested for domestic violence, *Violence Against Women* 6; 2000: 1190–203; J. Campbell, *Assessing Dangerousness* (Newbury Park: Sage); J. C. Campbell, P. W. Sharps, and N. Glass, Risk assessment for intimate partner violence,

in *Clinical Assessment of Dangerousness: Empirical Contributions*, eds. G.-F. Pinard and L. Pagani (New York: Cambridge University Press, 2000), 136–57.

14. L. Feder, Domestic violence and police response in a pro-arrest jurisdiction, *Women and Criminal Justice* 8; 1997: 79–98; A. Harrell, *Evaluation of Court-Ordered Treatment for Domestic Violence Offenders: Final Report* (Washington, DC: Institute for Social Analysis, 1991); M. Miller, E. Drake, and M. Nafziger, *What Works to Reduce Recidivism by Domestic Violence Offenders?* (Olympia: Washington State Institute for Public Policy, 2013), http://www.wsipp.wa.gov/ReportFile/1119/Wsipp_What-Works-to-Reduce-Recidivism-by-Domestic-Violence-Offenders_Full-Report.pdf (accessed August 25, 2015); L. Feder and D. B. Wilson, A meta-analytic review of court-mandated batterer intervention programs: Can courts affect abusers behavior? *Journal of Experimental Criminology* 1; 2005: 239–62; J. Babcock, C. E. Green, and C. Robie, Does batterers treatment work? A meta-analytic review of domestic violence treatment, *Clinical Psychology Review* 23; 2004: 1023–53; A. R. Klein, *Practical Implications of Current Domestic Violence Research: For Law Enforcement, Prosecutors and Judges* (Washington, DC: U.S. Department of Justice, 2009); L. Bennett, C. Call, H. Flett, and C. Stoops, *Program Completion, Behavioral Change, and Re-Arrest for the Batterer Intervention System of Cook County Illinois: Final Report to the Illinois Criminal Justice Information Authority* (Chicago: Illinois Criminal Justice Information Authority, 2005); M. Labriola, M. Rempel, and R. C. Davis, Do batterer programs reduce recidivism? Results from a randomized trial in the bronx, *Justice Quarterly* 25; 2008: 252–82; S. Jackson, L. Feder, D. R. Forde, R. C. Davis, C. D. Maxwell, and B. G. Taylor, Batterer intervention programs: Where do we go from here? *National Institute of Justice Special Report* (Washington, DC: U.S. Department of Justice, 2003). In this last evaluation, the researchers found that there was no improvement in all three programs evaluated in participants' attitudes toward domestic violence, but found that a longer program (26 weeks) in Brooklyn resulted in fewer official complaints lodged against those who completed the program. However, there is considerable controversy surrounding the impact of, and results for, men who drop out of these programs, and longer programs result in considerably higher rates of attrition. See J. L. Edleson, Groupwork with men who batter: What the research literature indicates, *VAWnet*, February 2012, http://www.vawnet.org/Assoc_Files_VAWnet/AR_GroupworkMenWhoBatter.pdf (accessed December 10, 2015). Edleson reviews the research in the past decade on intervention programs and asserts that they "have a positive impact on ending and reducing violence among men who participate in them" (3), but my review of the research on this topic suggests this claim is unsupported. He does not mention the large body of research contrary to this assertion, he includes Gondolf's (2004) assessment, which has been roundly and rightly criticized for

both its methodology and unwarranted rosy interpretations, and he presents some unlikely explanations for the limited success he finds. For example, he posits that positive results might be due to men who dropped out of these programs seeking treatment elsewhere (with success in that treatment), thus reducing the differences between the men who completed the programs being studied and those who did not complete them. Asserting that many (if any) offenders did this strains credibility. He also tends to overstate "positive" findings. For example, he characterizes Babcock, Green and Robie's (2004) meta-analytic review of treatment programs in the following manner: "The strongest results are found among studies using official records of subsequent police arrests and comparing those who complete the program to those who drop out of the program" (3). However, these "strong" results are characterized by the researchers themselves as having a "minimal impact on reducing recidivism beyond the effect of being arrested" (1023). He offers Feder and Wilson's (2005) research as another example of a meta-analysis showing the "strongest" positive effect, while the researchers themselves concluded that their results were mixed, and that, overall, their findings "raise serious doubts about the effectiveness of court-mandated batterer treatment programs" (239).

15. For an excellent overview of this body of research, see C. Mitchell, *Intimate Partner Violence: A Health-Based Perspective* (New York: Oxford University Press, 2009) or E. S. Buzawa, C. G. Buzawa, and E. Stark, *Responding to Domestic Violence: The Integration of Criminal Justice and Human Services*, 5th ed. (Thousand Oaks, CA: Sage, 2017).
16. See, for example, L. Feder and L. Dugan, *Testing a Court-Mandated Treatment Program for Domestic Violence Offenders: The Broward Experiment* (Washington, DC: National Institute of Justice, 2004).
17. L. K. Hamberger and J. E. Hastings, Court-mandated treatment of men who assault their pPartner, in *Legal Responses to Wife Assault: Current Trends and Evaluation,* ed. N. Zoe Hilton (Newbury Park, CA: Sage Publications, 1993), 188–229; Harrell, *Evaluation of Court-Ordered Treatment for Domestic Violence Offenders.*
18. R. Tolman and L. Bennett, A review of quantitative research on men who batter, *Journal of Interpersonal Violence* 5; 1990: 87–118.
19. C. J. Easton, D. L. Mandel, K. A. Hunkele, C. Nich, B. J. Rounsaville, and K. M. Carroll, A cognitive behavioral therapy for alcohol-dependent domestic violence offenders: An integrated substance abuse-domestic violence treatment approach (SADV), *American Journal on Addictions* 16; 2007: 24–31; W. Fals-Stewart, J. Golden, and J. A. Schumacher, Intimate partner violence and substance use: A longitudinal day-to-day examination, *Addictive Behaviors* 28; 2003: 1555–74; J. Friend, J. Langhinrichsen-Rohling, and B. H. Eichold, II, Same-day substance use in men and women charged with felony domestic violence offenses, *Criminal Justice and Behavior* 38; 2011: 619–33; D. G. Dutton and A. J. Starzomski, Borderline personality in perpetrators of

psychological and physical abuse, *Violence and Victims* 8; 1993: 327–37; A. E. Fruzzetti and E. R. Levensky, Dialectical behavior therapy for domestic violence, *Cognitive and Behavioral Practice* 7; 2000: 435–47; J. Waltz, Dialectical behavior therapy in the treatment of abusive behavior, *Journal of Aggression, Maltreatment and Trauma* 7; 2003: 75–103; D. G. Dutton, Trauma symptoms and PTSD-like profiles in perpetrators of intimate violence, *Journal of Traumatic Stress* 8; 1995: 299–316; A. A. Gerlock, Domestic violence and post-traumatic stress disorder severity for participants of a domestic violence rehabilitation program, *Military Medicine* 169; 2004: 470–4; D. R. Tollefson, K. Webb, D. Shumway, S. H. Block, and Y. Nakamura, A mind-body approach to domestic violence perpetrator treatment: Program overview and preliminary outcomes, *Journal of Aggression, Maltreatment and Trauma* 18; 2009: 17–45; D. A. Andrews, J. Bonta, and R. D. Hoge, Classification for effective rehabilitation: Rediscovering psychology, *Criminal Justice and Behavior* 17; 1990: 19–52.
20. M. Labriola, M. Rempel, C. S. O'Sullivan, and P. B. Frank, *Court Responses to Batterer Program Noncompliance: A National Perspective* (New York: Center for Court Innovation, 2010), https://www.ncjrs.gov/pdffiles1/nij/grants/230399.pdf (accessed July 30, 2015)
21. O. Kenyan, H. Rosenberg, B. Beili, M. Nir, S. Levin, A.Mor, I. Agabaria, and A. Tefelin, Beit Noam Residential program for violent men, *Journal of Aggression, Maltreatment and Trauma* 7; 2003: 207–36.
22. Ibid.
23. Ibid.
24. Ibid.
25. M. Levin-Rozalis, N. Bar-On, and H. Hartaf, A unique therapeutic intervention for abusive men at Beit Noam: Successes, boundaries and difficulties, *Journal of Social Work Research and Evaluation* 6; 2005: 25–45.
26. Ibid, 33.
27. M. A. Sumner, A different response to intimate partner violence, *Community Policing Dispatch*, September, 2014, http://cops.usdoj.gov/html/dispatch/09-2014/a_different_response_to_ipv.as\ (accessed November 4, 2015).
28. Ibid.
29. M. A. Sumner, Domestic violence initiative, *City of High Point, North Carolina*, 2014, http://www.highpointnc.gov/police/focus_deterrence/domestic_violence_initiative/index.cfm (accessed November 4, 2015).
30. M. A. Sumner, Offender focused domestic violence initiative: The first two years, *City of High Point, North Carolina*, 2014, http://www.highpointnc.gov/police/focus_deterrence/domestic_violence_initiative/docs/Offender_Focused_DV_Initiative_Report_Aug_2014.pdf (accessed November 4, 2015).
31. Ibid.
32. Ibid.
33. Ibid, 4.
34. Ibid, 5.

35. D. E. Elliott, P. Bjelajac, R. D. Fallot, L. S. Markoff, and B. G. Reed, Trauma-informed or trauma-denied: Principles and implementation of trauma-informed services for women, *Journal of Community Psychology* 33; 2005: 461–77; Washington Coalition of Sexual Assault Programs, *Creating Trauma-Informed Services: A Guide for Sexual Assault Programs and Their System Partners* (Olympia, Washington: Washington Coalition of Sexual Assault Programs, 2012).
36. Z. Lodrick, Psychological trauma—What every trauma worker should know, *The British Journal of Psychotherapy Integration* 4; 2007: 1–19.
37. C. Warshaw, C. M. Sullivan, and E. A. Rivera, *A Systemic Review of Trauma-Focused Interventions for Domestic Violence Survivors* (Washington, DC: National Center on Domestic Violence, Trauma & Mental Health, 2013).
38. M. A. Pico-Alfonso, M. Isabel Garcia-Linares, N. Celda-Navarro, C. Blasco-Ros, E. Echeburúa, and M. Martinez, The impact of physical, psychological, and sexual intimate male partner violence on women's mental health: Depressive symptoms, posttraumatic stress disorder, state anxiety, and suicide, *Journal of Women's Health* 15; 2006: 599–611; M. Ellsberg, H. A. Jansen, L. Heise, C. Watts, and C. Garcia-Moreno, Intimate partner violence and women's physical and mental health in the WHO multi-country study on women's health and domestic violence: An observational study, *Lancet* 371; 2008: 1165–72.
39. R. Campbell, M. R. Greeson, D. I. Bybee, and S. Raja, The co-occurrence of childhood sexual abuse, adult sexual assault, intimate partner violence, and sexual harassment: A mediational model of post-traumatic stress disorder and physical health outcomes, *Journal of Consulting and Clinical Psychology* 76; 2008: 194–207; M. Cascardi, K. D. O'Leary, and K. A. Schlee, Co-occurrence and correlates of posttraumatic stress disorder and major depression in physically abused women, *Journal of Family Violence* 14; 1999: 227–49; S. Pimlott-Kubiak and L. M. Cortina, Gender, victimization, and outcomes: Reconceptualizing risk, *Journal of Consulting and Clinical Psychology* 71; 2003: 528–39; N. P. Roberts, N. J. Kitchiner, J. Kenardy, and J. I. Bisson, Systematic review and meta-analysis of multiple-session early interventions following traumatic events, *American Journal of Psychiatry* 166; 2009: 293–301; E. Stark, *Coercive Control: How Men Entrap Women in Personal Life* (New York: Oxford University Press, 2007); M. P. Thompson, N. J. Kaslow, J. B. Kingree, A. Rashid, R. C. Puett, D. Jacobs, and A. Matthews, Partner violence, social support, and distress among inner-city African American women, *American Journal of Community Psychology* 28; 2000: 127–43.
40. R. E. Fleury, C. Sullivan, and D. I. Bybee, When ending the relationship doesn't end the violence: Women's experiences of violence by former partners, *Violence Against Women* 6; 2010: 1363–83.
41. For example, one common feature of PTSD treatment is to carefully trigger memories of the trauma in a safe situation in order to show the patient that they are now safe, and the physical and psychological reactions that come with the memory of the event are not necessary.

E. B. Foa, L. A. Zoellner, N. C. Feeny, E. A. Hembree, and J. Alvarez-Conrad, Does imaginal exposure exacerbate PTSD symptoms? *Journal of Consulting and Clinical Psychology* 70; 2002: 1022–8. See also, M. Crespo and M. Arinero, Assessment of the efficacy of a psychological treatment for women victims of violence by their intimate male partner, *The Spanish Journal of Psychology* 13; 2010: 849–63.

42. M. A. Dutton, D. Bermudez, A. Matas, H. Majid, and N. A. Laurenzo Myers, Mindfulness-based stress reduction for low-income, predominantly African American women with PTSD and a history of intimate partner violence, *Cognitive and Behavioral Practice* 20; 2013: 23–32; L. R. Snowden, Barriers to effective mental health services for African Americans, *Mental Health Services Research* 3; 2001: 181–7; C. Warshaw, C. M. Sullivan, and E. A. Rivera, A systemic review of trauma-focused interventions for domestic violence survivors. National Center on Domestic Violence, Trauma & Mental Health, 2013. Available at: http://www.nationalcenterdvtraumamh.org/wp-content/uploads/2013/03/NCDVTMH_EBPLitReview2013.pdf

43. K. M. Chard, An evaluation of cognitive processing therapy for the treatment of posttraumatic stress disorder related to childhood sexual abuse, *Journal of Consulting and Clinical Psychology* 73; 2005: 965–71; A. McDonagh, M. Friedman, G. McHugo et al., Randomized trial of cognitive-behavioral therapy for chronic posttraumatic stress disorder in adult female survivors of childhood sexual abuse, *Journal of Consulting and Clinical Psychology* 73; 2005: 515–24; D. M. Johnson, C. Zlotnick, and S. Perez, Cognitive behavioral treatment of PTSD in residents of battered women's shelters: Results of a randomized clinical trial, *Journal of Consulting and Clinical Psychology* 79; 2011: 542–51; E. S. Kubany, E. E. Hill, and J. A. Owens, Cognitive trauma therapy for battered women with PTSD: Preliminary findings, *Journal of Traumatic Stress* 16; 2003: 81–91; E. S. Kubany, E. E. Hill, J. A. Owens, C. Iannce-Spencer, M. McCaig, and K. J. Tremayne, Cognitive trauma therapy for battered women with PTSD (CTT-BW), *Journal of Consulting and Clinical Psychology* 72; 2004: 3–18; P. A. Resick, T. E. Galovski, M. O. Uhlmansiek, C. D. Scher, G. A. Clum, and Y. Young-Xu, A randomized clinical trial to dismantle components of cognitive processing therapy for posttraumatic stress disorder in female victims of interpersonal violence, *Journal of Consulting and Clinical Psychology* 76; 2008: 243–58.

44. National Center on Domestic Violence, Trauma & Mental Health, *Creating Trauma-Informed Services (Tip Sheet Series): A Trauma-Informed Approach to Domestic Violence Advocacy* (Washington, DC: National Center on Domestic Violence, Trauma & Mental Health, 2011).

45. Law enforcement officers tend to be a bit more attuned to dealing with traumatized people due to their experiences in the field. Court personnel are less experienced in dealing with trauma, which has led to an initiative to train them about the variety of normal reactions and behaviors they might encounter. See National Center on Domestic Violence, Trauma & Mental Health, *Trauma-Informed Legal Advocacy (TILA) Project*

(Washington, DC: National Center on Domestic Violence, Trauma & Mental Health, 2015), http://www.nationalcenterdvtraumamh.org/trainingta/trauma-informed-legal-advocacy-tila-project/ (accessed August 30, 2015).

46. L. A. Sherman and R. A. Berk, *The Minneapolis Domestic Violence Experiment* (Washington, DC: Police Foundation, 1984), http://www.policefoundation.org/wp-content/uploads/2015/07/Sherman-et-al.-1984-The-Minneapolis-Domestic-Violence-Experiment.pdf (accessed December 2, 2015).
47. J. Fagan, *Criminalization of Domestic Violence: Promises and Limitations* (Washington, DC: National Institute of Justice, 1995), https://www.ncjrs.gov/txtfiles/crimdom.txt?iframe=true&width=95%&height=95% (accessed December 4, 2015).
48. E. S. Buzawa and C. G. Buzawa, *Domestic Violence: The Criminal Justice Response* (Thousand Oaks, CA: Sage, 1990); R. I. Parnas, The police response to domestic disturbance, *Wisconsin Law Review* 31; 1967: 914–60; International Association of Chiefs of Police, *Training Key 16: Handling Disturbance Calls* (Washington, DC: International Association of Chiefs of Police, 1967).
49. E. S. Buzawa and C. G. Buzawa, *Domestic Violence: The Criminal Justice Response* (Thousand Oaks, CA: Sage, 1990), pp. 94–109.
50. R. Davis, Domestic violence and mandatory arrests. *PoliceOne News*, November 19, 2007, http://www.policeone.com/patrol-issues/articles/1457670-Domestic-violence-and-mandatory-arrests/ (accessed December 5, 2015).
51. The National Institute of Justice sponsored six such replications of the Minneapolis experiment beginning in 1986 with sites in Charlotte, North Carolina, Colorado Springs, Colorado, Miami-Dade County, Florida, Milwaukee, Wisconsin, and Omaha, Nebraska (a study was initiated in Atlanta, Georgia, but was not completed). A. Weisz, *Spousal Assault Replication Program: Studies of Effects of Arrest on Domestic Violence* (Harrisburg, PA: National Resource Center on Domestic Violence, November 2001), http://www.vawnet.org/applied-research-papers/print-document.php?doc_id=394 (accessed December 5, 2015); J. H. Garner and C. D. Maxwell, What are the lessons of the police arrest studies? *Journal of Aggression, Maltreatment and Trauma* 4; 2000: 83–114; J. D. Hirschel, I. W. Hutchinson, III, and C. W. Dean, The failure of arrest to deter spouse abuse, *Journal of Research in Crime and Delinquency* 29; 1992: 7–33; A. Pate and E. E. Hamilton, Formal and informal deterrents to domestic violence: The Dade County spouse assault experiment, *American Sociological Review* 57; 1992: 691–7.
52. C. D. Maxwell, J. H. Garner, and J. Fagan, The preventive effect of arrest on intimate partner violence: Research, policy, and theory, *Criminology and Public Policy* 2; 2002: 51–80.
53. M. P. Johnson, Patriarchal terrorism and common couple violence: Two forms of violence against women, *Journal of Marriage and the Family* 57; 1995: 283–94; R. M. Milardo, Gender asymmetry in common couple

violence, *Personal Relationships* 5; 1998: 423–38; R. P. Dobash, R. E. Dobash, M. Wilson, and M. Daly, The myth of sexual symmetry in marital violence, *Social Problems* 39; 1992: 71–91.
54. D. Hirschel, *Domestic Violence Cases: What Research Shows about Arrest and Dual Arrest Rates* (Washington, DC: Office of Justice Programs, 2008), 6, https://www.ncjrs.gov/pdffiles1/nij/222679.pdf (accessed December 6, 2015).
55. Ibid, 10.
56. J. Fagan, Cessation of family violence: Deterrence and dissuasion, *Crime and Justice: An Annual Review of Research* 11; 1989: 377–425.
57. D. Hirschel, *Domestic Violence Cases: What Research Shows about Arrest and Dual Arrest Rates* (Washington, DC: Office of Justice Programs, 2008), 6, https://www.ncjrs.gov/pdffiles1/nij/222679.pdf (accessed December 6, 2015).
58. Domesticshelters.org, Using GPS to track batterers, Domesticshelters.org, July 15, 2015, https://www.domesticshelters.org/domestic-violence-articles-information/using-gps-to-track-batterers#.VmNPmd_cbZU (accessed October 30, 2015).
59. Ibid.
60. S. V. Gies, R. Gainey, M. I. Cohen, E. Healy, D. Duplantier, M. Yeide, A. Bekelman, A. Bobnis, and M. Hopps, *Monitoring High-Risk Sex Offenders with GPS Technology: An Evaluation of the California Supervision Program, Final Report* (Washington, DC: National Institute of Justice, 2012), https://www.ncjrs.gov/pdffiles1/nij/grants/238481.pdf (accessed October 29, 2015).
61. For some reason, this effect did not hold in the South. Researchers attribute the difference with other regions to sampling anomalies.
62. The negative features noted by offenders included practical problems with the equipment, the stigma of being monitored as a domestic violence offender, and the transparency in their whereabouts.
63. Ibid.
64. Ibid.
65. A. Green, More states use GPS to track abusers, *New York Times*, May 8, 2009, http://www.nytimes.com/2009/05/09/us/09gps.html?_r=0 (accessed November 1, 2015).
66. S. H. Spencer, ACLU challenges GPS tracking for sex offenders, *Delaware Law Weekly*, May 13, 2015, http://www.delawarelawweekly.com/id=1202726172994/ACLU-Challenges-GPS-Tracking-for-Delaware-Sex-Offenders?slreturn=20151108142418 (accessed December 1, 2015).
67. M. Labriola, S. Bradley, C. S. O'Sullivan, M. Rempel, and S. Moore, *A National Portrait of Domestic Violence Courts, Final Report* (Washington, DC: U.S. Department of Justice, 2009), https://www.ncjrs.gov/pdffiles1/nij/grants/229659.pdf (accessed November 12, 2015).
68. Ibid, 80.
69. Ibid, 81.
70. Ibid, 81.
71. Ibid.

72. E. S. Buzawa, C. G. Buzawa, and E. Stark, *Responding to Domestic Violence: The Integration of Criminal Justice and Human Services*, 5th ed. (Thousand Oaks, CA: Sage, 2017); A. B. Cissner, M. Labriola, and M. Rempel, *Testing the Effects of New York's Domestic Violence Courts: A Statewide Impact Evaluation* (New York: Center for Court Innovation, 2013); N. A. Crowell and A. W. Burgess, *Understanding Violence Against Women* (Washington, DC: National Academy Press, 1996); R. R. Peterson, *The Impact of King's County Integrated Domestic Violence Court on Case Processing* (New York: New York City Criminal Justice Agency, 2014); R. R. Peterson, *Comparing the Processing of Domestic Violence Cases to Non-Domestic Violence Cases in New York City Criminal Courts: Final Report* (New York: New York City Criminal Justice Agency, 2001).
73. New York State Division of Criminal Justice Services, *New York State Domestic Violence Courts Program Fact Sheet* (New York: New York State Division of Criminal Justice Services, 2015), http://www.criminaljustice.ny.gov/ofpa/domviolcrtfactsheet.htm (accessed December 1, 2015); E. S. Buzawa, C. G. Buzawa, and E. Stark, *Responding to Domestic Violence: The Integration of Criminal Justice and Human Services*, 5th ed. (Thousand Oaks, CA: Sage, 2017).
74. L. Newmark, M. Rempel, K. Diffily, and K. Mallik-Kane, *Specialized Felony Domestic Violence Courts: Lessons on Implementation and Impacts from the Kings County Experience* (Washington, DC: Urban Institute, 2004), https://www.ncjrs.gov/pdffiles1/nij/grants/191861.pdf (accessed December 2, 2015).
75. Domestic Abuse Intervention Programs, What is the Duluth Model? http://www.theduluthmodel.org/about/index.html (accessed December 2, 2015).
76. Domestic Abuse Intervention Programs, Why the Duluth Model Works, http://www.theduluthmodel.org/about/why-works.html (accessed December 2, 2015).
77. For a comprehensive defense of critical findings about the Duluth Model, see M. Palmer and G. Barnes, *Countering Confusion about the Duluth Model* (Duluth, MN: Domestic Abuse Intervention Programs, 2015), http://www.theduluthmodel.org/pdf/CounteringConfusion.pdf (accessed December 1, 2015). For a very pointed criticism of the Duluth Model, see D. G. Dutton and K. Corvo, The Duluth model: A data-impervious paradigm and a failed strategy, *Aggression and Violent Behavior* 12; 2007: 658–67. Other research on the effectiveness of CCR: E. W. Gondolf, Theoretical research support for the Duluth model: A reply to Dutton and Corvo, *Aggression and Violent Behavior* 12; 2007: 644–57; E. L. Pence, Some thoughts on philosophy, in *Coordinating Community Responses to Domestic Violence: Lessons from Duluth and Beyond*, eds. M. F. Shepherd and E. L. Pence (Thousand Oaks, CA: Sage, 1999), 29–30; R. L. Pender, ASGW best practice guidelines: An evaluation of the Duluth model, *Journal for Specialists in Group* Work 37; 2012: 218–31; M. E. Asmus, T. Ritmeester, and E. L. Pence, Prosecuting domestic abuse cases in Duluth: Developing effective prosecution

strategies from understanding the dynamics of abusive relationships, *Hamline Law Review* 115; 1992: 115–27; E. L. Pence and M. Paymar, *Education Groups for Men Who Batter: The Duluth Model* (New York: Springer, 1993); E. L. Pence and M. F. Shepard, Integrating theory and practice: The challenge of the battered women's movement, in *Feminist Perspectives on Wife Abuse*, eds. K. Yllö and M. Bograd (Beverly Hills, CA: Sage, 1988), 282–98; M. F. Shepard, *Evaluation of the Educational Curriculum-Power and Control: Tactics of Men Who Batter* (Duluth, MN: Domestic Intervention Project, 1988); M. F. Shepard, *Visitation Center Evaluation* (Duluth, MN: Minnesota Program Development, 1991); M. F. Shepard, Predicting batterer recidivism five years after community intervention, *Journal of Family Violence* 7; 1992: 167–78; M. F. Shepard, Child visiting and domestic abuse, *Child Welfare* 4; 1992: 357–67; M. F. Shepard and J. C. Campbell, The abusive behavior inventory, *Journal of Interpersonal Violence* 7; 1992: 291–305; M. F. Shepard, D. Falk, with M. Raschick, *Final Report of the Evaluation of the Enhanced Domestic Abuse Intervention Project* (Atlanta, GA: Centers for Disease Control and Prevention, 2000); S. Jackson, L. Feder, D. R. Forde, R. C. Davis, C. D. Maxwell, and B. G. Taylor, *Batterer Intervention Programs: Where Do We Go from Here?* (Washington, DC: National Institute of Justice, 2003).

78. For a thoughtful discussion of the problems with the treatment aspect of the Duluth model, see M. Twohey, How can domestic abuse be stopped? *Chicago Tribune*, January 2, 2009, http://www.chicagotribune.com/news/chi-abusers-02-jan02-story.html (accessed December 3, 2015).
79. P. Cluss and A. Bodea, *The Effectiveness of Batterer Intervention Programs: A Literature Review and Recommendations for Next Steps* (Washington, DC: FISA Foundation, 2011).
80. This is a summary of the more methodologically sound work on batterer intervention programs: J. Babcock, C. E. Green, and C. Robie, Does batterers treatment work? A meta-analytic review of domestic violence treatment, *Clinical Psychology Review* 23; 2004: 1023–53.
81. T. Porter, A call to men, *TEDTalk*, December, 2010, http://www.ted.com/talks/tony_porter_a_call_to_men?language=en (accessed October 6, 2015).
82. For an interesting discussion about the intersection of masculinity and sports, see M. A. Messner, When bodies are weapons: Masculinity and violence in sport, *International Review for the Sociology of Sport* 25; 1990: 203–18; M. A. Messner and D. F. Sabo, *Sex, Violence and Power in Sports: Rethinking Masculinity* (Freedom, CA: Crossing Press, 1994).
83. Adapted from: A Call to Men, Ten things men and boys can do to break out of the man box, *Educate Yourself, A Call to Men: The Next Generation of Manhood*, n.d., http://www.acalltomen.org/educate (accessed October 6, 2015).
84. D. McConnell, *American Honor Killings: Desire and Rage mong Men* (New York, NY: Akashic Books, 2013); S. E. Hatty, *Masculinities, Violence, and Culture* (Thousand Oaks, CA: Sage, 2000); J. Archer, *Male Violence*

(New York, NY: Routledge, 1994); L. Bowker, *Masculinities and Violence* (Thousand Oaks, CA: Sage, 1998); R. W. Connell, *Masculinities* (Berkeley, CA: University of California Press, 1995); J. Hood-Williams, Gender, masculinities and crime: From structures to psyches, *Theoretical Criminology* 5; 2001: 37–60; M. S. Kimmel, *Manhood in America: A Cultural History* (New York: Free Press, 1996); M. S. Kimmel and M. A. Messner, eds., *Men's Lives* (Boston, MA: Allyn and Bacon, 2001); J. W. Messerschmidt, *Nine Lives: Adolescent Masculinities, the Body, and Violence* (Boulder, CO: Westview Press, 2000); M. Miedzian, *Boys Will Be Boys: Breaking the Link between Masculinity and Violence* (New York, NY: Doubleday, 1991); K. Polk, *When Men Kill: Scenarios of Masculine Violence* (New York, NY: Cambridge University Press, 1994); E. H. Thompson, Jr., The maleness of violence in dating relationships: An appraisal of stereotypes, *Sex Roles* 24; 1991: 261–78; C. West and D. H. Zimmerman, Doing gender, *Gender and Society* 1; 1987: 125–81; M. Wilson and M. Daly, Competitiveness, risk taking, and violence: The young male syndrome, *Ethology and Sociobiology* 6; 1985: 59–73; M. Wolfgang and F. Ferracuti, *The Subculture of Violence: Towards an Integrated Theory in Criminology* (New York, NY: Routledge, 2010).

85. J. Katz, Reconstructing masculinity in the locker room: The mentors in violence prevention project, *Harvard Educational Review* 65; 1995: 163–75.
86. Texas Council on Family Violence, *Guide to Engaging Men and Boys in Preventing Violence Against Women and Girls* (Austin, TX: Men's Nonviolence Project, 2009).
87. See the Men Stopping Violence webpage for a wealth of information, http://www.menstoppingviolence.org/ (accessed December 12, 2015).

Appendix I: Power and Control Wheel

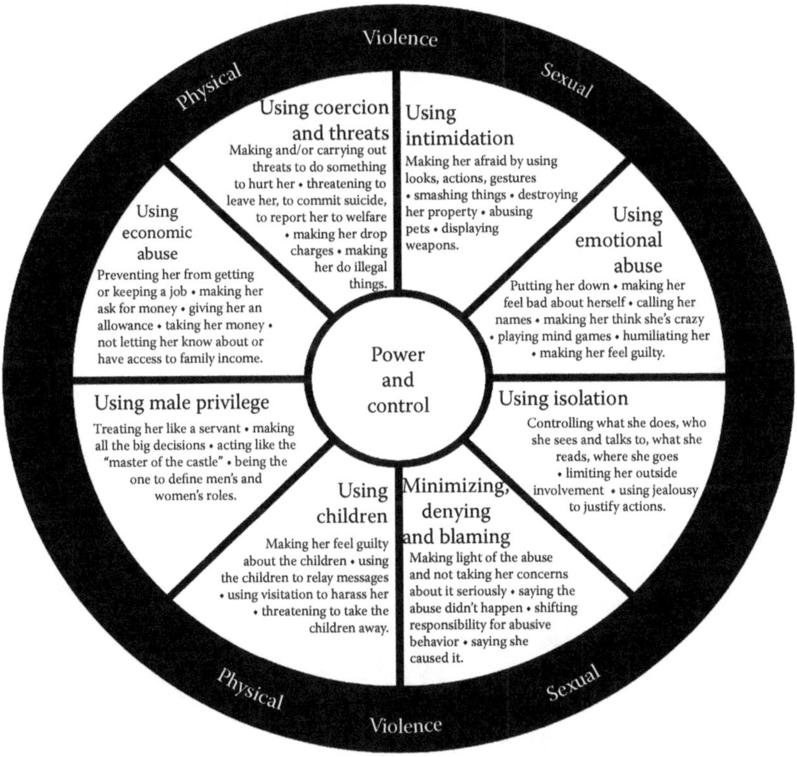

Source: Domestic Abuse Intervention Project, 202 East Superior Street, Duluth, Minnesota 55802, 218-722-2781, www.duluth-model.org

Appendix II: Danger Assessment Tool

Several risk factors have been associated with increased risk of homicides (murders) of women and men in violent relationships. We cannot predict what will happen in your case, but we would like you to be aware of the danger of homicide in situations of abuse and for you to see how many of the risk factors apply to your situation.

Using the calendar, please mark the approximate dates during the past year when you were abused by your partner or ex-partner. Write on that date how bad the incident was according to the following scale:

1. Slapping, pushing; no injuries and/or lasting pain
2. Punching, kicking; bruises, cuts and/or continuing pain
3. "Beating up"; severe contusions, burns, broken bones
4. Threat to use weapon; head injury, internal injury, permanent injury
5. Use of weapon; wounds from weapon

(If any of the descriptions for the higher number apply, use the higher number.)

Mark Yes or No for each of the following. ("He" refers to your husband, partner, ex-husband, ex-partner or whoever is currently physically hurting you.)

____ 1. Has the physical violence increased in severity or frequency over the past year?

____ 2. Does he own a gun?

____ 3. Have you left him after living together during the past year?

3a. (If have never lived with him, check here____)

____ 4. Is he unemployed?

____ 5. Has he ever used a weapon against you or threatened you with a lethal weapon?

(If yes, was the weapon a gun? ____)

____ 6. Does he threaten to kill you?

____ 7. Has he avoided being arrested for domestic violence?

____ 8. Do you have a child that is not his?

____ 9. Has he ever forced you to have sex when you did not wish to do so?

____ 10. Does he ever try to choke you?

____ 11. Does he use illegal drugs? By drugs, I mean "uppers" or amphetamines, "meth," speed, angel dust, cocaine, "crack," street drugs, or mixtures.

____ 12. Is he an alcoholic or problem drinker?

____ 13. Does he control most or all of your daily activities? For instance: Does he tell you who you can be friends with, when you can see your family, how much money you can use, or when you can take the car? (If he tries, but you do not let him, check here: ____)

____ 14. Is he violently and constantly jealous of you? (For instance, does he say "If I can't have you, no one can.")

____ 15. Have you ever been beaten by him while you were pregnant? (If you have never been pregnant by him, check here: ____)

____ 16. Has he ever threatened or tried to commit suicide?

____ 17. Does he threaten to harm your children?

____ 18. Do you believe he is capable of killing you?

____ 19. Does he follow or spy on you, leave threatening notes or messages, destroy your property, or call you when you don't want him to?

____ 20. Have you ever threatened or tried to commit suicide?

____ Total "Yes" Answers

Thank you. Please talk to your nurse, advocate or counselor about what the Danger Assessment means in terms of your situation.

J. C. Campbell, Danger Assessment, 2004, http://www.dangerassessment.org (accessed December 10, 2015).

J. C. Campbell, D. W. Webster, and N. Glass, The danger assessment: Validation of a lethality risk assessment instrument for intimate partner femicide, *Journal of Interpersonal Violence* 24; 2009: 653–74.

Appendix III: Biderman's Chart of Coercion

SYNOPSIS WRITTEN BY RUS ERVIN FUNK

This short article describes a breakdown of various forms of coercion used in a variety of settings. Looking at a number of forms of oppression and violence, this model has real implications for looking at the forms of coercion used in domestic violence.

Isolation is seen as consisting of three forms:

- Depriving an individual of social support which effectively inhibits that person's ability to resist
- Makes the individual dependent on the perpetrator
- Develops an intense concern with the "self" of the perpetrator(s)

Monopolization of perception is another tactic used and likewise consists of three forms or consequences:

- Fixes attention of the victim on the immediate predicament—fostering introspection (which inhibits one's ability to hope, plan or resist)

- Eliminates competing stimuli (which reinforces the omnipotence of the perpetrator)
- Frustrates actions not consistent with compliance

Induced debility and exhaustion. The victim becomes worn out by the levels of tension and fear, and by constantly attempting to "read" the perpetrator and their behavior; while simultaneously avoid expressing fear, sorrow or rage to avoid further consequences from the perpetrator.

Occasional indulgences which reinforce the omnipotence of the perpetrator and provides motivation for compliance.

Devaluing the person through words and actions. This can result in

- Creating fear of freedom and dependence on the perpetrator
- Reinforcing feelings of helplessness
- Developing lack of faith in their own capabilities

These tactics and the consequences are seen commonly in forms of torture and can provide a framework to better understand the impact of domestic violence.

Available at http://www.ncdsv.org/images/Chart_of_Coercion1.pdf

Appendix IV: Safety Plan

Name: ______________________________ **Date:** _____________

The following steps represent my plan for increasing my safety and preparing in advance for the possibility for further violence. Although I do not have control over my partner's violence, I do have a choice about how to respond to him/her and how to best get myself and my children to safety.

STEP 1: Safety during a violent incident. *Women cannot always avoid violent incidents. In order to increase safety, battered women may use a variety of strategies.*

I can use some of the following strategies:

A. If I decide to leave, I will __________________________. (*Practice how to get out safely. What doors, windows, elevators, stairwells or fire escapes would you use?*)

B. I can keep my purse and car keys ready and put them (*loction*) ______________________________ in order to leave quickly.

C. I can tell __________________________ about the violence and request that she or he call the police if she or he hears suspicious noises coming from my house.

D. I can teach my children how to use the telephone to contact the police, the fire department and 911.

E. I will use ______________________________ as my code with my children or my friends so they can call for help.

F. If I have to leave my home, I will go to ________ ______________________________. (*Decide this even if you don't think there will be a next time.*)

G. I can also teach some of these strategies to some or all of my children.

H. When I expect we're going to have an argument, I'll try to move to a place that is low risk, such as ______________________________. (*Try to avoid arguments in the bathroom, garage, kitchen, near weapons or in rooms without access to an outside door.*)

I. I will use my judgment and intuition. If the situation is very serious, I can give my partner what he/she wants to calm him/her down. I have to protect myself until I/we are out of danger.

STEP 2: Safety when preparing to leave. *Battered women frequently leave the residence they share with the battering partner. Leaving must be done with a careful plan in order to increase safety. Batterers often strike back when they believe that a battered woman is leaving a relationship.*

I can use some or all of the following strategies:

A. I will leave money and an extra set of keys with ____________________ so I can leave quickly.

B. I will keep copies of important documents or keys at ____________________.

C. I will open a savings account by ____________________, to increase my independence.

D. Other things I can do to increase my independence include: ______________________________.

E. I can keep change for phone calls on me at all times. I understand that if I use my telephone credit card, the following month's phone bill will show my batterer those numbers I called after I left. To keep my phone communications confidential, I must either use coins, or I might ask to use a friend's phone card for a limited time when I first leave.

F. I will check with ________________ and ________________ to see who would be able to let me stay with them or lend me some money.

G. I can leave extra clothes or money with ________________.

H. I will sit down and review my safety plan every ________________ in order to plan the safest way to leave the residence. ________________ (domestic violence advocate or friend's name) has agreed to help me review this plan.

I. I will rehearse my escape plan and, as appropriate, practice it with my children.

STEP 3: Safety in my own residence. *There are many things that a woman can do to increase her safety in her own residence. It may be impossible to do everything at once, but safety measures can be added step by step.*

Safety measures I can use are as follows:

A. I can change the locks on my doors and windows as soon as possible.

B. I can replace wooden doors with steel/metal doors.

C. I can install security systems including additional locks, window bars, poles to wedge against doors, an electronic system, etc.

D. I can purchase rope ladders to be used for escape from second floor windows.

E. I can install smoke detectors and fire extinguishers for each floor of my house/apartment.

F. I can install an outside lighting system that activates when a person is close to the house.

G. I will teach my children how to make a collect call to me and to ________________ (name of friend, etc.) in the event that my partner takes the children.

H. I will tell the people who take care of my children, which people have permission to pick up my children and that my partner is not permitted to do so. The people I will inform about pick-up permission include:

________________ (name of school)
________________ (name of babysitter)
________________ (name of teacher)
________________ (name of Sunday-school teacher)
________________ (name[s] of others)

I can inform ____________ (neighbor) and ______________ (friend) that my partner no longer resides with me and that they should call the police if he is observed near my residence.

STEP 4: Safety with an Order of Protection. *Many batterers obey protection orders, but one can never be sure which violent partner will obey and which will violate protective orders.* I recognize that I may need to ask the police and the courts to enforce my protective order.

The following are some steps I can take to help the enforcement of my protection order:

A. I will keep my protection order ___________ (location). *Always keep it on or near your person. If you change purses, that's the first thing that should go in the new purse.*
B. I will give my protection order to police departments in the community where I work, in those communities where I visit friends or family, and in the community where I live.
C. *There should be county and state registries of protection orders that all police departments can call to confirm a protection order.* I can check to make sure that my order is on the registry. The telephone numbers for the county and state registries of protection orders are the following: _______________________ (county) and __________________________ (state).
D. I will inform my employer; my minister, rabbi, etc.; my closest friend; and ______________________ that I have a protection order in effect.
E. If my partner destroys my protection order, I can get another copy from the clerk's office.
F. If the police do not help, I can contact an advocate or an attorney and file a complaint with the chief of the police department or the sheriff.
G. If my partner violates the protection order, I can call the police and report the violation/contact.

STEP 5: Safety on the job and in public. *Each battered woman must decide if and when she will tell others that her partner has battered her and that she may be at continued risk. Friends, family and coworkers can help to protect women. Each woman should carefully consider which people to invite to help secure her safety.*

I might do any or all of the following:

A. I can inform my boss, the security supervisor and ______________________ at work.

B. I can ask ______________________ to help me screen my telephone calls at work.

C. When leaving work, I can ______________________ ______________________.

D. If I have a problem while driving home, I can ______________________ ______________________.

E. If I use public transit, I can ______________________ ______________________.

F. I will go to different grocery stores and shopping malls to conduct my business and shop at hours that are different from those I kept when residing with my battering partner.

G. I can use a different bank and go at hours that are different from those kept when residing with my battering partner.

STEP 6: Safety and drug or alcohol use. *Most people in this culture use alcohol. Many use mood-altering drugs. Much of this is legal, although some is not. The legal outcomes of using illegal drugs can be very hard on battered women, may hurt her relationship with her children, and can put her at a disadvantage in other legal actions with her battering partner. Therefore, women should carefully consider the potential cost of the use of illegal drugs. Beyond this, the use of alcohol or other drugs can reduce a woman's awareness and ability to act quickly to protect herself from her battering partner. Furthermore, the use of alcohol or other drugs by the batterer may give him an excuse to use violence. Specific safety plans must be made concerning drugs or alcohol use.*

If drug or alcohol use has occurred in my relationship with my battering partner, I can enhance my safety by some or all of the following:

A. If I am going to use, I can do so in a safe place and with people who understand the risk of violence and are committed to my safety.

B. If my partner is using, I can ______________________ ______________ and/or ______________________ ______________________.

C. To safeguard my children I might ______________________

____.

STEP 7: Safety and my emotional health. *The experience of being battered and verbally degraded by partners is usually exhausting and emotionally draining. The process of building a new life takes much courage and incredible energy.*

To conserve my emotional energy and resources and to avoid hard emotional times, I can do some of the following:

A. If I feel down and am returning to a potentially abusive situation, I can ______________________________

____.

B. When I have to communicate with my partner in person or by telephone, I can ______________________________

____.

C. I will try to use "I can …" statements with myself and be assertive with others.

D. I can tell myself, "______________________________" whenever I feel others are trying to control or abuse me.

E. I can read ______________________________ to help me feel stronger.

F. I can call ______________ and ______________ for support.

G. I can attend workshops and support groups at the domestic violence program or ______________________ to gain support and strengthen relationships.

STEP 8: Items to take when leaving. *When women leave partners, it is important to take certain items. Beyond this, women sometimes give an extra copy of papers and an extra set of clothing to a friend just in case they have to leave quickly.*

Money: Even if I never worked, I can take money from jointly held savings and checking accounts. If I do not take this money, he can legally take the money and close the accounts.

Items on the following lists with asterisks by them are the most important to take with you. If there is time, the other items might be taken, or stored outside the home. These items might best be placed in one location, so that if we have to leave in a hurry, I can grab them quickly. When I leave, I should take:

*Identification for myself *Children's birth certificate
*My birth certificate *Social security cards
*School and vaccination records *Money
*Checkbook, ATM card *Credit cards
*Key—house, car, office *Driver's license and registration *Medications *Copy of protection order
*Welfare identification, work permits, green cards
Passport(s), divorce papers
Medical records—for all family members
Lease/rental agreement, house deed, mortgage payment book
Bank books, insurance papers
Address book
Pictures, jewelry
Children's favorite toys and/or blankets
Items of special sentimental value

Telephone numbers I need to know

Police/sheriff's department (local)—911 or ________________
Police/sheriff's department (work) ________________________
Police/sheriff's department (school) ______________________
Prosecutor's office ____________________________________
Battered women's program (local) ________________________
National Domestic Violence Hotline: 800-799-SAFE (7233)
800-787-3224 (TTY)
www.ndvh.org
County registry of protection orders ______________________
State registry of protection orders ________________________
Work number ____
Supervisor's home number ______________________________

I will keep this document in a safe place and out of the reach of my potential attacker.

Review date: ______________________

From *Domestic Violence Personalized Safety Plan* (Austin, TX: National Center on Domestic and Sexual Violence), http://www.ncdsv.org/images/DV_Safety_Plan.pdf (accessed May 6, 2015).

The National Center on Domestic and Sexual Violence features many useful resources that you can access at www.ncdsv.org

Index

www.ingramcontent.com/pod-product-compliance
Lightning Source LLC
LaVergne TN
LVHW021037011026
849160LV00009BA/688
* 9 7 8 1 4 9 8 7 7 3 5 9 1 *